CURSES, HEXES, & SPELLS

THE WEIRD AND HORRIBLE LIBRARY

Other titles sure to chill and thrill you:

MAGICIANS, WIZARDS, & SORCERERS
by Daniel Cohen

MONSTERS FROM THE MOVIES
by Thomas G. Aylesworth

MUMMIES
by Georgess McHargue

POLTERGEISTS: HAUNTINGS AND THE HAUNTED
by David C. Knight

SEANCES & SPIRITUALISTS
by Christine Andreae

THE SOOTHSAYER'S HANDBOOK—
A GUIDE TO BAD SIGNS & GOOD VIBRATIONS
by Elinor Lander Horwitz

VAMPIRES
by Nancy Garden

WEREWOLVES
by Nancy Garden

WITCHES, WIT AND A WEREWOLF
by Jeanne B. Hardendorff

CURSES, HEXES, & SPELLS

by DANIEL COHEN

J. B. LIPPINCOTT COMPANY
PHILADELPHIA AND NEW YORK

ACKNOWLEDGMENTS

Pictures appearing on page 24, courtesy of the Library of Congress; pages 11, 16, 32, 36, 38, 45, 48, 94, from *Devils, Demons, Death and Damnation* by Ernst and Johanna Lehner (Dover Publications, Inc., New York, 1971); pages 43, 70, 71, 106, courtesy of the New York Public Library Picture Collection; pages 61, 62, courtesy of the Peabody Museum of Salem; page 63, courtesy of the Atlantic Mutual Companies; page 51, courtesy of the Department of the Navy; page 75, from *Curious Myths of the Middle Ages* by Sabine Baring-Gould (Longmans, Green, London, 1897); page 78, from *Symbols, Signs & Signets* by Ernst Lehner (Dover Publications, Inc., New York, 1950); page 99, courtesy of the School of Wicca, Salem, Missouri; page 115, from *Amulets and Talismans* by E. A. Wallis Budge (University Books, New York, 1961).

U.S. Library of Congress Cataloging in Publication Data

Cohen, Daniel.
  Curses, hexes & spells.

  (The Weird and horrible library)
  SUMMARY: Recounts curses on families, creatures, places, wanderers, and ghosts. Also describes amulets and talismans which provide protection.
  Bibliography: p.
  1. Blessing and cursing—Juvenile literature. 2. Charms—Juvenile literature. 3. Legends—Juvenile literature. [1. Blessing and cursing. 2. Charms. 3. Witchcraft] I. Title.
GR600.C63 1974   133.4   74-6425
ISBN-0-397-31493-0   ISBN-0-397-31494-9 (pbk.)

TO GENE AND JAN MODJESKI

CONTENTS

I - THE OLD FAMILY CURSE

Should a father's mortal sins
Be visited on babykins?
—Ring Lardner

OUR LOVE of the weird and horrible is nothing new. Throughout history people have been fascinated by grisly stories—the ghastlier they were the better people seemed to like them. Even the ancient Greeks, regarded by many as the most civilized people ever, had their share of gruesome tales and blood-drenched accounts of horrible murder and hideous revenge. The fifth century B.C. tragic poet Aeschylus used a popular story of the curse laid upon the family of an ancient king named Atreus as the basis for a cycle of three plays called the *Oresteia*.

We don't know how much of the story of the "Curse of the House of Atreus" is historically factual. The tale was an old one even before Aeschylus' time. It had been passed on from generation to generation by word of mouth since a time before the Greeks possessed a written language. It had been told and retold so often, and in so many different forms, that any historical basis it might have had was lost. Even the details of the story vary considerably in the many versions that have survived. But it is not unreasonable to assume that, like so many other Greek myths, the story had at least some basis in fact. It seems fitting that we should begin our examination of curses, hexes, and spells with this ancient tale.

The story begins long before Atreus himself was born. It begins with one Tantalus who, according to mythology, was one of the god Zeus' many children by mortal women. Tantalus was king of Phrygia, a Greek-ruled country in Asia Minor. He was favored by the gods above all other mortals and was given the honor of being allowed to dine with them on Mount Olympus. But for some reason, perhaps envy, Tantalus was not satisfied by the honors the gods bestowed upon him. At the banquet he stole some of their nectar and ambrosia.

After being allowed to dine on Olympus, Tantalus invited the gods to a feast at his home. In preparing for this feast Tantalus did something so horrible that the poets of the Greeks were at a loss for an explanation of the act. He had his only son Pelops killed, boiled in a great cauldron, and served up as the main course at his feast for the gods. Says the celebrated classicist Edith Hamilton in her book *Mythology*, "Apparently he was driven by a passion of hatred against them which made him willing to sacrifice his son in order to bring upon them the horror of being cannibals." The Greek gods were a violent lot—and not at all moral by our standards—but they considered cannibalism an unspeakable crime.

The Olympians knew at once the nature of the horrible feast they had been offered and refused to eat. That is, all except one, the goddess Demeter, who was either less observant or hungrier than the rest. She took a bite out of Pelops' shoulder.

The gods decreed that Tantalus should suffer a punishment befitting his crime, one which would serve as a warning to all men that the gods could not be insulted with impunity. He was placed in the middle of a pool in Hades, beneath heavily laden fruit trees. When he tried to bend down and drink the water it immediately drained away into the ground. When he tried to reach up and take

Tantalus, cursed by the gods to spend eternity consumed by hunger and thirst yet unable to reach the fruit that dangled just above his head or the water in which he stood.

some fruit to eat the wind blew the branches of the trees out of his reach. Since he was descended from Zeus, Tantalus was immortal and thus was condemned to stand, consumed by thirst and hunger, for all eternity, while the drink and food remained forever just beyond his reach. Tantalus' fate gave rise to our word "tantalize."

His son Pelops was restored to life by the gods, who fashioned an ivory shoulder for him to replace the part bitten off by Demeter.

This story is so brutal that some later poets protested that it wasn't true. The poet Pindar called it: "A tale decked out with glittering lies against the word of truth. Let a man not speak of cannibal deeds among the blessed gods." Glittering lies or not, the story was repeated and added to.

The restored Pelops took a fancy to a dangerous lady named Hippodamia. Her father, Oenomatis, had agreed to give his daughter in marriage to anyone who could beat him in a chariot race. Losers were to be punished by death. Oenomatis had two magic horses to insure his victories, and fifteen suitors had already been killed. Pelops was not willing to risk his life in such a dangerous contest, so he bribed Oenomatis' chariot master, Myrtilus, to loosen one of the chariot wheels. Pelops was an easy victor in the race. Later Pelops killed the chariot master in order to be rid of an embarrassing accomplice. Myrtilus died cursing Pelops. It happened that Myrtilus also had divine connections—his father was the god Hermes. Hermes saw to it that the curse was carried out. Some say that the curse started here, while others assert that Tantalus' original crime was the starting point for the curse. Whatever the reason, the rest of the family history is extremely gloomy.

Tantalus' daughter Niobe married the powerful king of Thebes. She had more than a touch of her father's arrogance and demanded that the people of Thebes worship her rather than the gods. For this affront the god Apollo and the goddess Artemis, both excellent archers, shot down all of Niobe's sons and daughters before her eyes. The sight so horrified her that she turned to stone.

Pelops had two sons, Atreus and Thyestes, and they hated each other. When Thyestes took Atreus' wife as his mistress, Atreus planned a revenge worthy of his grandfather. He pretended to be reconciled with Thyestes and invited him to a feast. He then had two of Thyestes' young sons killed, cooked, and served to their father. When Thyestes found out what he had eaten, he cursed the descendants of Atreus with all the might he could summon. The gods, too, were offended by the revolting crime, and the sun was said to have hidden itself so as not to have to cast light on such a dreadful deed. So yet another curse was added to this already roundly cursed family. Eventually Atreus was killed by Aegisthus, another of Thyestes' sons.

The curse continued to work in the next generation. Atreus had two sons, Agamemnon and Menelaus. Their story is the best-known part of the tale, for it is recounted by Homer in his epic poems, the *Iliad* and the *Odyssey*. Menelaus, king of Sparta, suffered the relatively minor fate of having his wife Helen, the most beautiful woman in the world, carried off by Paris, son of the king of Troy and, incidentally, the handsomest man in the world. To get his wife back, Menelaus enlisted the aid of his brother Agamemnon to make war on Troy. In order to gain a favorable wind to carry his ships to Troy, Agamemnon sacrificed his daughter Iphigenia. The Greeks then sailed off to Troy, and after a war that dragged on for seven years, they were victorious.

During the long years of the Trojan War, Agamemnon's wife Clytemnestra brooded over the death of her daughter. She had also taken a lover to console her—Aegisthus, the murderer of Atreus. When the victorious Agamemnon returned home he walked right into a trap. He did this despite the fact that he had with him a prophetess named Cassandra, who correctly foretold what was going to happen. Cassandra, however, was burdened by a curse of her own—she could make accurate predictions, but she was fated never to be believed. So Agamemnon accepted an invitation to a banquet, where Clytemnestra and Aegisthus killed him and the unlucky Cassandra.

And so the curse descended upon yet another generation of the House of Atreus. Agamemnon had two surviving children, a boy, Orestes, and a girl, Electra. Clytemnestra and Aegisthus were well aware of the family history of revenge and would have killed the boy had they been able to get their hands on him. But he managed to escape and hide. Electra stayed behind nursing a desperate hatred for her mother and her mother's lover. Finally, Orestes came back. He disguised himself as a messenger bringing news of his own death. This was a welcome message for Clytemnestra, and Orestes was allowed into the house. Once inside, he killed both Clytemnestra and Aegisthus with Electra serving as a willing accomplice.

After this incredible series of atrocities there were very few members of the House of Atreus left, yet the curse still had to work itself out. For the crime of killing his mother, Orestes was tormented by avenging spirits called the Furies. For years he wandered about like a madman. Finally the Furies were satisfied—and the Curse of the House of Atreus came to an end.

With the obviously mythological elements stripped away from this doleful tale, we can see it as the story of a large and powerful family that lived in a barbaric age. The members of the House of Atreus killed one another regularly, not an uncommon practice in a warrior society, but their arrogance and brutality were so great that they shocked even their violence-prone contemporaries. People must have assumed that they also offended the gods or transgressed the laws of nature and were therefore fated to suffer.

The Greeks were strong believers in fate. It didn't matter that Clytemnestra was justified in hating Agamemnon or that Orestes, in turn, was justified in hating his mother. They were fated to commit the crimes they did and to be punished for them. What we would consider justice or fair play had nothing to do with the situation. Indeed, the idea that the sins of the fathers are visited upon the sons is supremely unjust. But the curse is a supernatural or divine force beyond such human considerations.

The tales surrounding the House of Atreus are so complicated that one suspects a number of originally separate stories were combined over the years into the single grand cycle of myths. It is hard to be sure what the Greeks themselves—that is the sophisticated and cultured Greeks of that civilization's Golden Age during the fifth century B.C.—thought of such tales. They were, after all, ancient to them too. Many of these Greeks would probably no longer have regarded the curse as a sign of the direct intervention of the gods. Many doubted the existence of the gods altogether, or at the very least doubted the ability of the gods to alter the course of human affairs directly. Yet the idea of a curse, be it caused by divine intervention, fate, or whatever, was something which continued to fascinate them.

The Greeks weren't the only people fascinated by the idea of a curse that passed from generation to generation. The ancient Hebrews believed very strongly that their god would impose such curses on disobedient individuals. On Mount Sinai the Lord told Moses, "I, the Lord your God, am a jealous god. I punish the children for the sins of the fathers to the third and fourth generations of those who hate me" (Exod. 23:5–6).

In a very real sense, the ancient Hebrews regarded all mankind as an accursed race. In Genesis, when God discovers that Adam has disobeyed his instructions and eaten the forbidden fruit, he drives Adam and Eve from the Garden of Eden, saying to Adam: "Because you have listened to your wife and have eaten from the tree which I forbade you, accursed shall be the ground on your account" (Gen. 3:17).

This curse, commonly called the Fall of Man or Original Sin, condemned us all to toil, suffering, and eventual death. The Hebrews never made a great deal of the Fall. The Christians, however, did. The idea of Original Sin as the cause of all our woes figures importantly throughout much of Christian history. By the time of the Protestant Reformation in the sixteenth century the great religious leader John Calvin (1509–1564) declared man to be "totally depraved." A small minority of "the elect" would be saved by "the Free Grace of God," but the vast majority of mankind would be condemned to eternal damnation—and there was nothing, not piety, prayer, nor good works, that the damned could do about it. Again, there was no justice as we would usually define the term. Most of mankind was to suffer eternal torment for the sin of our

Adam, Eve, and the Tree of Knowledge represented as Death. From a woodcut by Jost Amman, first printed in 1587.

remote ancestor Adam. Those to be saved were to be saved for no reason other than that God willed it.

America's foremost theologian of colonial times, Jonathan Edwards (1703–1758), used to terrify his congregation with descriptions of what God was going to do to them. In one of his most famous sermons, "Sinners in the Hands of an Angry God," Edwards said:

> And though He will know that you cannot bear the weight of omnipotence treading upon you, yet He will not regard that, but He will crush out your blood, and make it fly, and it shall be sprinkled on His garments, so as to stain all His raiment. He will not only hate you, but He will have you in the utmost contempt; no place shall be fit for you but under His feet to be trodden down as the mire of the streets.

Edwards' sermons were said to have driven many of his hearers to despair and even suicide. Yet his view of mankind as an accursed race was the prevailing theological view in the America of that day. This grim view has softened considerably since Edwards' time.

If all of the sons and daughters of Adam were cursed, then no particular individual or family need suffer the wrath of God more ferociously than any other. Yet, almost immediately after the description of the Fall of Adam in the Bible, we find God placing a special, more familiar type of curse on one of Adam's sons. This is the curse placed upon Cain for the murder of his brother Abel:

> Now you are accursed, and banished from the ground which has opened its mouth wide to receive your brother's blood, which you have shed. When you till the ground, it will no longer yield you its wealth. You shall be a vagrant and a wanderer on earth (Gen. 4:11–12).

When Cain protested that people could kill a wanderer at will, "The Lord answered him, 'No: If anyone kills Cain, Cain shall be avenged sevenfold.' So the Lord put a mark on Cain, in order that anyone meeting him should not kill him" (Gen. 4:15). Thus the idea that a cursed person may bear a special physical mark entered our culture.

Shortly after God cursed Cain, there is a description in the Bible of Noah cursing his youngest son Ham and all of Ham's descendants. This particular story has had one extremely unfortunate side effect. Throughout history it has been common practice for conquerors to label the conquered—especially the darker races, for Ham was said to be dark—the accursed descendants of Ham. This seemed a perfect excuse for subjugating others, though doubtless different excuses would have been found if the story of Ham had not appeared in the Bible.

It is obvious that the idea that a family or an entire race can be cursed for the sin of a remote ancestor is a familiar one in Western society. Warring families regularly cursed one another and attributed their own misfortunes to curses placed upon them by their enemies. Every time a prominent family suffered a series of reverses rumors of a curse were likely to pop up.

In 1972 Hans Holzer, a prolific writer on psychic subjects, wrote a book called *The Habsburg Curse*. The book is about the curse that supposedly dogged the ancient and noble Habsburg family. The Habsburgs first entered recorded history during the tenth century as members of the minor aristocracy of Central Europe. By shrewdly marrying into families better placed than theirs, the ambitious Habsburgs rose from obscurity. At one time or another members of the family were rulers of most of Europe and large tracts of the New World as well. They hung tenaciously on to power until the breakup of the Austro-Hungarian empire at the end of World War I.

Holzer traces the beginning of the curse to the actions of one of the Habsburg dukes during the thirteenth century. The duke raped a girl and then had her imprisoned when she became troublesome. The girl, Holzer says, placed a curse on the family, and this accounts for the string of disasters that followed.

Marie Antoinette, the queen of France who was beheaded during the French Revolution, was a Habsburg. The Habsburg archduke Maximilian went to Mexico in 1863 and, with the backing of the French, managed to set up a short-lived "empire" there. But his plans miscarried badly, and in 1867 he was captured by Mexican rebels and executed. The Crown Prince Franz Ferdinand had the misfortune to get himself assassinated in the Yugoslavian city of Sarajevo by Serbian nationalists. This was the incident which led to World War I, the conflict that finally brought an end to the Habsburg dynasty.

A more genuinely mysterious death came to Crown Prince Rudolf, the only son of Emperor Franz Joseph. Rudolf had fallen passionately in love with Baroness Marie Vetsera. On January 29, 1889, both Rudolf and his mistress were found dead in his hunting lodge at Mayerling near Vienna. A double suicide was the announced explanation for the deaths, but mystery has always surrounded the tragedy, and there have been frequent hints of murder. The imperial Habsburgs had all the evidence relating to the deaths destroyed or suppressed. The tragedy at Mayerling remains one of history's strangest cases.

And these are just some of the more recent and better-known Habsburg disasters. Without a doubt the Habsburgs have had their share of spectacular bad luck. On the other hand, they spent nearly nine hundred years at the center of European power, and that was very often a dangerous place to be. Though the Habsburgs sometimes failed, they clearly succeeded even more often, or they would not have remained so powerful for so long. It might be equally possible to make out a case for the idea that the Habsburgs were a specially favored family by concentrating on those in the family who lived long and successful lives and ignoring or passing quickly over the tragedies.

Deciding whether or not a family is well and truly cursed should be a matter of statistics. In any large group of people, pure chance would dictate that a certain percentage will be what we call "fortunate" whereas a certain percentage will be "unfortunate." If the Habsburgs or any other supposedly cursed family had a considerably higher percentage of unfortunates than chance would allow, then perhaps we might be correct in thinking in terms of a curse. But no one has ever worked out an adequate statistical model for the distribution of fortune and misfortune. With so many variables and unknowns in the equation such a model would be a statistician's nightmare, if not a downright impossibility.

Let us consider for a moment the factor of what we might call luck. Sir Aleister Hardy, a British biologist and a pioneer in psychical research, once speculated that there exists a factor of luck in the universe. He first got the idea during a period in his life when he played a lot of cards. There were times when he always won and others when he always lost. He found that among his card-playing companions there were those who won consistently and those who lost just as consistently. The distribution of good and bad luck seemed to defy probability. Statisticians, of course, would reply that it didn't. The explanation, they would say, lay in the fact that Hardy's sample—that is, the number of persons observed at some task such as card playing over a certain period—simply wasn't large enough, and therefore was statistically worthless. But Hardy was never sure, and most of us certainly have had the feeling that some people are just plain luckier than others.

Might this "luck" factor apply to families as well? Might it not account for the apparent curse upon certain families? This is, of course, unproven and probably unprovable speculation. But it is interesting to think about.

An almost certain reason for at least some family-curse tales is the existence of hereditary diseases. In past ages, before people understood the science of genetics, a particular illness or defect that appeared often, but unpredictably, in any particular family might be looked upon as the manifestation of a curse. Families which tended to intermarry would be the worst victims of hereditary diseases. The genes for most hereditary diseases are recessive, and therefore the disease appears in an individual only if both parents carry the gene. The parents themselves may show no signs of the disease. Since aristocratic families were likely to practice intermarriage with close relatives, they often fell victim to their own desire to keep their blood "pure." This may help to account for the fact that curse stories about aristocratic families are more common than those about commoners.

The best-known hereditary disease in royal families in modern times is the bleeder's disease, hemophilia. The hemophiliac lacks a clotting factor in his blood, so even a minor injury can be extremely dangerous. There was nothing that could be done for hemophiliacs until fairly recently. It is ironic to note that the disease was spread throughout the royal families of Europe by that most fortunate of modern monarchs, Queen Victoria of England. Victoria herself did not suffer from hemophilia; on the contrary, throughout her long life she enjoyed exceptionally good health. But she did pass the trait on to her numerous children and grandchildren and through them to most of the royal houses of Europe.

Victoria's granddaughter Alexandra, who became the wife of Tsar Nicholas II of Russia, had a hemophiliac son. The anxiety the boy's sickness caused his mother led to her being dominated by the notorious monk Rasputin, who seemed to have some ability to affect the course of the disease in the child.

Nicholas, Alexandra, and their children were executed during the Russian Revolution. In an era when less was known about hereditary diseases it would have been possible to imagine that the Russian royal family had been struck with a curse. Alexandra, who was an exceptionally superstitious woman, looked upon her son's affliction and the other family misfortunes as a form of divine punishment.

As we pointed out, noble families are more famous for their curses than commoners, though presumably the poor have a greater percentage of misfortunes than the rich. There are two basic reasons for this. First is that noble families are better known. Only a small number would ever hear of murders, suicides, and other untimely deaths in the family of a shoemaker, but everyone would hear of the same events if they struck the family of the king. Then there is the belief that misfortune is the natural lot of the poor, whereas the rich and wellborn should be favored. If they are not, then something out of the ordinary, perhaps the supernatural agency of a curse, must be in operation. Perhaps too, there is the feeling that so terrible yet grand a thing as a curse, which suspends the usual laws of nature, is reserved for the powerful and the famous.

In his play *Julius Caesar* Shakespeare wrote:

When beggars die, there are not comets seen;
The Heavens themselves blaze forth the death of princes.

So it seems to be with family curses—they rarely bother with the lowly, a fact for which all we lowly should, I assume, be grateful.

When America abandoned the aristocratic standards of the Old World for the egalitarian standards of democracy, much of the impetus went out of the old family-curse idea. There were naturally local traditions of family curses, but nothing on the grand scale of the curse of the House of Atreus or the Habsburg curse. In most parts of modern America, people know so little about their families that it would be hard to get a good family-curse tradition started. It is, therefore, more than a little ironic that the family history most reminiscent of a family-curse story during the latter half of the twentieth century is that of the closest thing to a royal family America has ever had—the Kennedy family.

The Kennedys have inspired more affection, more controversy, and certainly more interest than any other American family within recent memory. Even the English, who are notoriously tradition minded, are less interested in their royal family than we Americans have been in the Kennedys. Very few in America, indeed in the entire Western world, are unaware of the fabulous successes and appalling tragedies that have marked the lives of the children of Joseph and Rose Kennedy.

Foremost among the tragedies was, of course, the assassination of President John F. Kennedy in 1963. This was followed by the assassination of Senator Robert Kennedy during the presidential primary campaign of 1968. Preceding these two tragedies was the death during World War II of the eldest of the Kennedy sons, Joseph, Jr. Other members of the Kennedy family have been involved in serious accidents, become seriously ill, or have been handicapped. The youngest Kennedy son, Edward, broke his back in a plane crash. Then he had an automobile accident on the island of Chappaquiddick, and the girl who was riding in his car was killed. When Kennedy made a nationally televised speech concerning the accident, he said that shortly after it happened he was struck by the thought that his family was afflicted with some sort of terrible curse. He rejected the idea, but many others have not.

Have the Kennedys had more tragedies than can be accounted for by the normal course of events? Is there a Kennedy curse? Statistics, as was already pointed out, are virtually unusable in such cases. But it is well to remember that the Kennedys are a large

family and that America is, alas, a violent country. A number of presidents before John Kennedy were assassinated, and politicians, especially those who inspire strong feelings, have increasingly become the targets of would-be assassins.

A problem with curses is that if one starts looking for evidence of them, one is bound to find it if one looks hard enough and far enough. In the years following the assassination of President Kennedy there was talk of the many "mysterious" deaths of those connected with the event. The most notable killing was that of assassin Lee Harvey Oswald. This killing was shown live on national television. Oswald's killer, Jack Ruby, died in prison of cancer a few years later. And there were others connected with the case in one way or another who died under mysterious circumstances—or circumstances which seemed mysterious when thought of in connection with the assassination. The suspicious looked upon the string of deaths as evidence of a conspiracy, though no two people ever seemed able to agree as to just what sort of conspiracy it was. The superstitious saw in these deaths the workings of an obscure, but lethal curse.

The assassination of President Kennedy raised the specter of another "curse," this one not connected with the Kennedy family, but rather with the institution of the presidency. This is the so-called twenty-year curse. A bizarre but undeniable fact is that all

A presidential curse? All the presidents elected at twenty-year intervals, starting in 1840, either have been assassinated or have died in office. From left to right: William Henry Harrison, elected 1840, died in office; Abraham Lincoln, elected to first term 1860, assassinated at start of second term; James A. Garfield, elected 1880, assassinated; William McKinley, elected to second term 1900, assassinated; Warren G. Harding, elected 1920, died in office; Franklin D. Roosevelt, elected to third term 1940, died at start of fourth term; John F. Kennedy, elected 1960, assassinated.

of the presidents elected at intervals of twenty years, starting with the election of 1840, either have been assassinated or have died in office.

The record is ominous. The first United States president to die in office was William H. Harrison, who died shortly after he was elected in 1840. The first president to be assassinated was Abraham Lincoln, elected in 1860, just twenty years after Harrison's election. In 1880 James A. Garfield was elected; he was also assassinated, as was William McKinley, elected in 1900. Warren G. Harding was elected in 1920, and he died in office. Franklin D. Roosevelt was elected in 1940 and died in office. Then, of course, there was John F. Kennedy, elected in 1960 and assassinated.

There was only one president who died in office but was not elected in this twenty-year cycle. He was Zachary Taylor, elected in 1848. The only two presidents elected in the twenty-year cycle who did not die in office were Thomas Jefferson, elected in 1800, and James Monroe, reelected in 1820, both before the 1840 starting point of the cycle.

This string of dreadful coincidences, if that is what they are, is extraordinary, though not as extraordinary as it appears at first glance. Several of the presidents who were assassinated or died were elected to more than one term. This upsets the statistical neatness of the cycle. Lincoln gets into the cycle on the basis of his first election in 1860. He was assassinated at the start of his second term. President McKinley was first elected in 1896, but gets into the cycle on the basis of his reelection in 1900. Franklin Roosevelt, who was elected to four terms, gets into the cycle on the basis of his third term. He died at the start of his fourth.

Another factor which must be weighed is that three out of the seven presidents died from natural causes. Since men are generally elected to the presidency when they are well into middle age, and since the pressures of the job create a drain on health, the death of men holding the office should not be surprising. Both presidents Woodrow Wilson and Dwight D. Eisenhower became critically ill while in office. Eisenhower recovered, but Wilson was virtually incapacitated for the final months of his presidency and died shortly after leaving office.

Taking all of this into consideration, and perhaps throwing in a bit of guesswork as well, one mathematician came up with the conclusion that the odds against such a string of deaths occurring by chance are 100 to 1. These are long odds, but improbable things sometimes happen.

Yet most of us find it difficult to ascribe such a series of deaths to chance alone. We are not comfortable with the concept of blind and impersonal chance. It seems more satisfying to think of the deaths as the result of a curse. Why do we so often feel this way? I can only offer a personal guess. For whatever it may be worth, here it is. When an awesome and terrible event like the death of a king or president takes place, we would like to believe that the event has some meaning, even if the meaning is an evil one.

For most of us it is less terrifying to contemplate a universe in which the sins of the fathers are visited upon the totally innocent sons than it is to contemplate a universe ruled entirely by blind and capricious chance. If the course of American history can be significantly altered by a lucky shot fired by a half-mad and not particularly competent assassin, then this seems to many an awful universe indeed. No, in the face of that conclusion, a curse seems far preferable. At least it is something one can depend upon.

But let us leave the gloomy subject of family curses and the like on a somewhat lighter note. There is little in the history of such curses that can be called genuinely humorous. But there is one tale that is so curious that it has become a particular favorite of mine. The story comes down to us from medieval times and may be entirely the result of some storyteller's imagination. It combines a curse with a werewolf story, though this werewolf was unusual in that it was normally quite harmless and really rather noble.

There was a knight in the French province of Brittany who possessed the ability to change into a wolf whenever he took his clothes off and change back into human form when he put them on again. He would often go out into the woods at night, take off his clothes, and run harmlessly around in his wolf form. But one night his faithless wife spied on his nocturnal rovings. Figuring out what was going on, she stole his clothes and hid them. Thus the knight was condemned to remain in wolf form. The werewolf was later captured by the king's huntsmen, but since he seemed such a gentle and intelligent animal the king made a pet of him.

Some months later the knight's wife and her lover visited the king's palace, and the pet wolf suddenly went wild. It attacked the pair and bit off the woman's nose. The king was astonished that his usually tame pet would react so violently for no apparent reason. He correctly suspected that the fault lay with the humans, not with the wolf. He had them arrested and the wife quickly confessed what she had done. The knight's clothes were restored to him, and he was again able to resume his human form. The wife was banished and cursed by the king, the curse being that all of her daughters would be born without noses, as a reminder of how the werewolf had punished their mother's crime.

II - ACCURSED CREATURES

"Footprints?"
"Footprints."
"A man's or a woman's?"
Dr. Mortimer looked strangely at us for an instant, and his voice sank almost to a whisper as he answered:
"Mr. Holmes, they were the footprints of a gigantic hound!"
    –Arthur Conan Doyle, The Hound of the Baskervilles

THE CLASSIC CURSE TALE of modern times, and possibly of all times, is the Sherlock Holmes story, *The Hound of the Baskervilles*. The background to the mystery is the curse brought down on the Baskerville family by the evil Hugo Baskerville. Hugo was supposed to have been pursuing an innocent girl across the lonely moors when he was attacked and killed by a supernatural beast in the shape of a gigantic black hound. Since the death of Hugo other members of the Baskerville family were also said to have met violent and mysterious deaths on the moors. Holmes is called into the case in order to protect Sir Henry Baskerville, surviving heir to the family estate and fortune.

The Hound of the Baskervilles is entirely fictional, the creation of the fertile imagination of Sir Arthur Conan Doyle. By the novel's end the great Holmes has laid the fears of the surviving Baskerville to rest by finding a perfectly natural explanation for all of the apparently supernatural happenings. But it isn't the explanation that sticks in our minds after reading the story; it is the curse of the Baskervilles itself. Nor did Arthur Conan Doyle invent the idea of a family or an individual being pursued by some sort of demon or evil spirit in animal form. His description of the finding of the body of Hugo Baskerville so thoroughly captures the mood of many ancient and widely believed tales of animal demons that it bears repeating:

> The moon was shining bright upon the clearing, and there in the centre lay the unhappy maid where she had fallen, dead of fear and fatigue. But it was not the sight of her body, nor was it that of the body of Hugo Baskerville lying near her, which raised the hair upon the heads of these three dare-devil roysterers, but it was that, standing over Hugo, and plucking at his throat, there stood a foul thing, a great black beast, shaped like a hound, yet larger than any hound that ever mortal eye has rested upon. And even as they looked the thing tore the throat out of Hugo Baskerville, on which, as it turned its blazing eyes and dripping jaws upon them, the three shrieked with fear and rode for dear life, still screaming, across the moor. One, it is said, died that very night of what he had seen, and the other twain were but broken men for the rest of their days.

The demon hound is not just a Conan Doyle creation either. The ancient Greek magician Apollonius of Tyana was reported to have rid a city of a plague by exorcising a demon in the shape of a huge black dog. It was said that the famous sixteenth-century magician Cornelius Agrippa was always accompanied by a black dog, believed by many to be a demon, from which he gained his magical knowledge. Then there is the black dog of Newgate, a monstrous creature that appeared mysteriously in the courtyard of the notorious prison shortly before every hanging.

Creatures of one sort or another figure prominently in accounts of supernatural evil. Some species possess reputations for evil and were believed to have been specially cursed. Others, like the fictional hound of the Baskervilles, are agents of curses. Still others like the black cat that crosses your path are omens of evil to come.

Of all the world's creatures, the one that has most universally been regarded with fear and loathing is the snake. The fact that the venom of many snakes is poisonous has not helped their reputation, but mankind's attitude toward the serpent seems more visceral than reasoned.

The Bible unhesitatingly lists the snake as the world's evilest animal. "The serpent was more crafty than any wild creature that the Lord God had made" (Gen. 3:1). After the serpent tempts Eve to eat of the forbidden fruit, God curses the serpent (Gen. 3:15):

> Because you have done this you are accursed more than all cattle and all wild creatures. On your belly you shall crawl, and dust you shall eat all the days of your life. I will put enmity between you and the woman, between your brood and hers. They shall strike at your head, and you shall strike at their heel.

In the Old Testament view, the serpent was a supreme symbol of evil, an undying enemy of the human race. Through a complicated process of myth-making the snake was transformed into another and more potent symbol of evil, the dragon. Actually, in ancient times the dragon was a large snake. The word comes from the Greek, and ancient Greek descriptions of dragons are quite clearly based upon exaggerated accounts of African or Indian pythons. The mythology of northern Europe also contains many tales of dragons. Just exactly

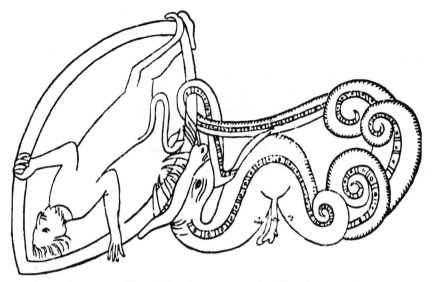

An evil spirit swallowed by the Dragon of Hell. After a miniature in an English manuscript of the twelfth century.

how the dragon idea reached Europe we cannot say, but if one looks at very early drawings and carvings of dragons it is obvious that these dragons too are large snakes.

Along the way, though, the dragon picked up wings, legs, and a whole host of supernatural characteristics, like the ability to breathe fire.

In the New Testament this snake-dragon became Satan himself. By the time we reach the Book of Revelation, the final book of the New Testament, we find this phrase: "So the great dragon was thrown down, that serpent of old that led the whole world astray, whose name is Satan, or the Devil—thrown down to the earth, and his angels with him" (Rev. 12:9).

Despite this very clear identification of the Devil as a serpent-dragon, he was rarely portrayed as one. Satan was most commonly identified with another animal, the goat. But more about goats shortly.

In the mythology of northern Europe many places said to be cursed were supposed to be guarded by a monster, usually a dragon. Folk tales told of dragons guarding treasures hidden deep within hollow hills or in the ruins of ancient castles. In Ireland and Scotland deep lakes were often rumored to be inhabited by monsters called, among other things, "worms." These creatures guarded the lakes and dragged the unwary to watery graves. The hardiest of these ancient water monsters is Scotland's Loch Ness Monster. A lot of people still believe that the Scottish loch is inhabited by a serpentine monster. Today, however, the Loch Ness Monster no longer inspires fear, merely curiosity.

The serpent as the agent of a curse can be seen most clearly in the story of the curse which was said to have afflicted the family of Lord Lambton of County Dorset in England. According to folklore the curse started around 1420. Young John Lambton, heir to the title, neglected his religious duties and went fishing in a nearby river on Sundays rather than going to church. One Sunday he hooked into something that struggled fiercely on the end of his line. A passing stranger asked, "What sport?" To which John Lambton replied, "Why truly I think I've caught the Devil!" When Lambton finally managed to pull the creature in he found it to be a "worm of most unseemly and disgusting appearance." He had never seen anything like it before and hoped never to see its likes again. He flung the thing into a well and tried to forget about it. For centuries this well was known as Worm Well, and the hill near where it stood, Worm Hill.

After this experience John Lambton gave up his loose ways and went off to join the Crusades in the Holy Land. But the "worm" that he had so thoughtlessly tossed into the well did not die. It grew into a first-class monster that was large enough to terrify the countryside and could not be killed by ordinary means. If cut in two it would miraculously reassemble itself. (Folklore attributes the same ability to snakes.)

When John Lambton returned from the Holy Land he found the family estate under siege. His father, old Lord Lambton, was virtually a prisoner in the castle, while the monster ruled the countryside. Several knights had already lost their lives in an attempt to kill the Lambton Worm.

Realizing that the creature could not be killed without supernatural aid, John Lambton consulted a witch. She said that he should stud his armor with spear blades and put his trust in his crusading sword. But she added a warning: After killing the monster John Lambton also had to kill the next living thing that he saw, or he would bring a curse upon his family.

The young knight in his spear-studded armor sallied forth and killed the monster without much trouble. But the story does not end there. Sir John had arranged to sound his hunting horn as soon as the worm was killed so that a hound could be released, which he would kill in accordance with the instructions given to him by the witch. However, old Lord Lambton was so overjoyed at hearing the signal that his son had overcome the monster that he forgot about the plan and rushed out of the hall in order to greet him. Thus, the first living thing John Lambton saw was his own father. Patricide was unthinkable, so John Lambton went back to the witch, who told him that the penalty for disobeying her command was that no Lord of Lambton for nine descending generations would die in his bed.

As it turned out a lot of them didn't. John Lambton's son Robert was drowned. Sir William Lambton, commander of a regiment of foot soldiers, was slain at the Battle of Marston Moor, and his son died at the head of a troop of dragoons at Wakefield in 1643. There were others who met untimely ends. The ninth descending generation from the original Sir John Lambton was Henry Lambton, a member of parliament who died, apparently from natural causes, while riding across New Bridge. So the curse of the Lambton family was fulfilled.

While the serpent and by implication the dragon are specifically cursed by God in the Bible, there are a large number of other creatures that wound up with a reputation for being cursed. Pagans often worshiped animal gods or feared evil spirits in animal form. When these pagans were converted to Christianity they didn't really abandon their beliefs in these various supernatural beings. Instead, they lumped them all as among the creatures damned by God and banished to the infernal regions or some equally distant and gloomy place. The trouble was that the creatures wouldn't stay banished; they kept creeping out of the darkness to terrify the new Christians.

Take, for example, the Anglo-Saxon epic *Beowulf*. This work was written down in Christian times, but it is basically a pagan story with only the most superficial veneer of Christianity. The chief villain of the tale is a monster called Grendel. Grendel is a natural killer, described as "drooling with spit, stinking and hairy." Just exactly what, if anything aside from a nightmare, originally inspired Grendel we don't know. This fiend and his folk were said to inhabit the dismal swamps and marshes, having been sent there by God along with the ghouls, dragons, lemurs, and other creatures that had been cursed and outlawed.

Not all cursed creatures were quite as horrible as Grendel, however. Monkeys and apes were regarded as cursed by medieval Christians, yet they never inspired much horror. The monkey's problem, as far as Christians were concerned, was that it looked too much like a man. It looked almost like a caricature, an obscene parody of humanity. Since man was made in the image of God and the monkey was a mockery of man, then the monkey must also be a

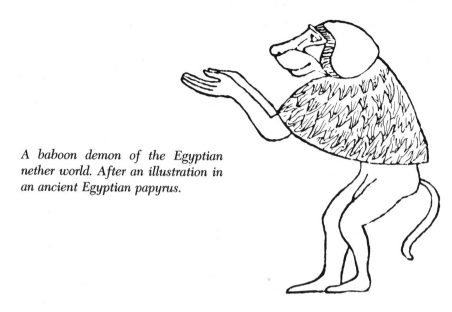

A baboon demon of the Egyptian nether world. After an illustration in an ancient Egyptian papyrus.

mockery of God and hence a creature of the Devil. There was some attempt to portray monkeys and apes as demons. As late as the sixteenth century Martin Luther used the words "apes" and "demons" interchangeably. But the characterization never really caught on. It was hard for people to think of the monkey as evil—foolish perhaps, but not evil.

The common folk finally decided that monkeys and apes were some debased form of humanity, fallen even lower than man himself, but not really the spawn of the infernal regions. As fellow sufferers, men tended to look upon monkeys and apes with indulgence and sympathy. During the Middle Ages "ape" was a common synonym for "drunk."

The Middle Ages are often portrayed as an era of great Christian piety, but this view can be misleading. The common folk often took enormous liberties with their religion. There grew up a whole host of folk tales which were not merely unscriptural, but downright blasphemous. Among them was this popular tale of how the apes came to be. After expelling Adam and Eve from the Garden of Eden, God visited them to see how they were doing. God asked Eve how many children she had. Eve had so many that she was afraid that God would think she was enjoying her newfound pleasures of the flesh too much, so she hid some of her children. God naturally knew this and, as punishment, placed a curse on those hidden children. Some were to become demons and the others apes.

While the ape may have been an object of tolerant amusement, the cat, like the snake, often inspired a supernatural dread in the medieval European. This represented a radical change of status for the cat. Among the ancient Egyptians cats were worshiped as divine. Living cats were prized by their owners above all their other possessions. A Greek traveler in Egypt during the fifth century B.C. reported with great astonishment that when an Egyptian's house burned down, he was more anxious to rescue his cats than anything else. When an Egyptian's favorite cat died, its owner went into deep mourning and shaved his eyebrows as a sign of respect.

Just how the cat was changed from a pagan divinity to a Christian demon is not altogether clear. According to one theory the cat figured prominently in the rites of the cult of Diana, one of the many mystery religions that flourished in the later days of the Roman empire. According to this theory many of these ancient cults, particularly the cult of Diana, survived the conversion of the Roman world to Christianity by going underground. Ultimately they became part of that collection of pagan and heretical beliefs and magical practices that has been given the name witchcraft.

Whether or not this theory of the origin of European witchcraft beliefs is true, it is a fact that the cat and the witch have been intimately associated with each other in the public mind since the Middle Ages. Usually the cat was treated as a familiar. A familiar is a demon or other form of evil spirit sent by Satan to aid the witch in

A wizard riding to a sabbat on a cat. From a sixteenth-century manuscript.

her evil deeds. The familiar might take many forms, but the most commonly reported was that of a cat.

The bond between a witch and her cat familiar was sealed with the witch's own blood. W. Oldfield Howley cites several cases in *The Cat in the Mysteries of Magic and Religion*. A witch tried at Windsor, England, in 1579 confessed to possessing a demon in the shape of a black cat "whereby she is aided in her witchcrafte, and she daiely feedeth it with Milke, mingled with her owne bloud." At another trial held in Essex a few years later evidence was given of a cat familiar who would come to the witch during the night "and suckle bloud of her upon her arms and other places of her body." When a group of accused witches of Huntingdonshire were brought to trial in 1646, one of the women explained how she had been given a cat by a witch and told that if she would deny God "and affirme the same by her bloud, then whomsoever she cursed and sent the Cat unto them, they should dye shortly after." This she had agreed to do and, pricking her finger with a thorn, had given it to the cat to lick.

Not only did witches possess cats as familiars that aided them in working their magic, but witches were also credited with the ability to change into various animal forms. Among the most commonly reported forms was that of a cat. Isobel Gowdie, dubbed queen of the Scottish witches, was tried and confessed in April of 1622. Her confession was given freely and without resort to torture, a rather unusual event in witchcraft trials. Her confession is also one of the most complete and bizarre on record, giving full details of a witches' sabbat and describing a visit to fairyland. Isobel Gowdie has handed down the magical formula by which she transformed herself into a cat and back again. The spell has to be repeated three times.

> I shall goe intill any catt
> Wit sorrow, and sych, and a blak shott;
> And I shall goe in the Divellis nam,
> Ay quhill I com hom againe.

In order to return to human form it was necessary to say:

> Catt, Catt God send thee a blak shott.
> I am in a cattis liknes just now,
> But I sal be in womanis liknes ewin now.
> Catt, Catt God send thee a blak shott.

Belief in the cat's supernatural ability to do evil has carried over into the present day. A modern occultist named Dion Fortune reported being "desperately afflicted with black cats" sent by one of her occult opponents.

Another side to the cat's reputation for being supernaturally evil is its long-standing connection with vampirism. While the witches freely offered their blood to cat familiars for the power the familiars might give them, there is an ancient belief that cats also sucked the blood of unwilling victims, that, in fact, cats were vampires. This belief seems even to predate the idea of cats as witches' familiars, indeed to predate the concept of witchcraft itself. According to Hebrew folklore Adam had a wife before Eve. Her name was Lilith, and she left paradise because she refused to submit to Adam. Since that time she has haunted the night as a demon and vampire. The Sephardic Jews believed that Lilith, in the form of a huge black cat called El Broosha, sucked the blood of newborn infants.

The ancient belief that cats represent some sort of mortal danger to infants persists in a somewhat altered form today. New mothers are often warned not to allow cats to sleep in an infant's room for fear that the cat might "suck" an infant's breath or smother the child. Few realize that the belief stretches back to Jewish legends of Lilith as a vampire cat.

Another belief was that cats or demons in cat form were able to turn the recently dead into vampires. Great care was always taken to keep cats out of a room in which the corpse of a person was laid out. Behind this fear was the idea that the cat was a demon which could possess the fresh body. Any cat that wandered into a room where there was a body was immediately killed if it could be caught. If the cat wasn't disposed of the result might be terrible as this seventeenth-century account quoted by Howley illustrates:

Johannes Cuntius, a citizen and alderman of Pentach,

in Silesia, when about sixty years of age, died somewhat suddenly, as the result of a kick from his horse. At the moment of his death a black cat rushed into the room, jumped on the bed and scratched violently at his face. Both at the time of his death and that of his funeral a great tempest rose—the wind and snow made men's bodies quake and their teeth chatter in their heads. The storm is said to have ceased with startling suddenness as the body was placed under the ground. Immediately after the burial, however, stories began to circulate of the appearance of a phantom which spoke to people in the voice of Cuntius. Remarkable tales were told of the consumption of milk from jugs and bowls, of milk being turned into blood, of old men soiled with blood, and poultry killed and eaten. Eventually it was decided to disinter the body. It was found that all the bodies buried above that of Cuntius had become putrefied and rotten, but his skin was tender and florid, his joints by no means stiff, and when a staff was put between his fingers they closed around it and held it fast in their grasp. He could open and shut his eyes, and when a vein in his leg was punctured the blood sprang out as fresh as that of a living person. This happened after the body had been in the grave for about six months. Great difficulty was experienced when the body was cut up and dismembered by the order of the authorities, by reason of the resistance offered; but when the task was completed and the remains consigned to the flames, the spectre ceased to molest the natives or interfere with their slumbers or health.

Today we inevitably associate the bat with the vampire. But most

people who really believed in vampires associated them with the cat
or the wolf, another animal that has inspired a host of beliefs about
its evil powers.

The bat always had a bad reputation in Europe. It was a creature
of the night, and it tended to inhabit remote and gloomy places like
caves and deserted buildings. But there was no clear connection of
the bat with vampirism until Hernan Cortez and other conquista-
dors brought back tales of blood-sucking (or, to be accurate,
blood-drinking) bats that they had found living in the New World.
Still, it wasn't until the publication of Bram Stoker's novel *Dracula*
near the end of the nineteenth century that bats became an
inevitable part of vampire lore. Now there is no separating the two.
How incongruous it seems to imagine Bela Lugosi turning into a cat!

While there are numerous descriptions of witches turning
themselves into cats and other creatures, the accounts of witches
using their magical powers to turn other people into animals are
relatively rare during the Middle Ages. There is, of course, the tale
of "The Frog Prince," the handsome prince who is turned into a
frog by a witch's spell and who can be restored to human form only
by the love of a beautiful princess. The story of "Beauty and the
Beast" concerns a similar plight of another handsome prince. But
these stories appear to be entirely fictional. Any folk beliefs that
they represent are those of much earlier times. The Greek myths are
filled with such tales. One appears in Homer's *Odyssey* where the
witch Circe turns Odysseus' crew into a herd of swine by putting a
magical potion in their drinks.

The votaries of the Dianic cult were rumored to possess the
power to turn human beings into animals. At least one survival of
this belief seems to have cropped up in medieval tales about
witches. Howley has found a sculptured stone panel at the entrance
of Lyons Cathedral which "pictures a witch riding a man she has
changed into a goat. She is whirling a cat around her unfortunate

A witch riding a man she has changed into a goat and whirling a cat around her victim's head. From a panel in Lyons Cathedral.

victim's head, so that it may tear his face with its claws and is apparently on her way to a Sabbat meeting."

Modern films and books about the supernatural use cats, bats, snakes, and other creatures as symbols of evil, but the goat is hardly ever used. Yet in medieval times there was no more powerful and persistent symbol of the forces of evil—yes, of the Devil himself—than the goat. Why the goat? It is not a nocturnal creature like the cat or bat, nor is it poisonous like the snake, or potentially dangerous like the wolf. There would seem nothing about this ill-tempered, but normally inoffensive plant eater to inspire associations with evil. Who would be afraid of a weregoat? Yet time after time in the witch trials the accused asserted that the Devil appeared to them in the form of a great black goat.

In pagan times the goat did not have the reputation of being evil; it was a symbol of fertility. In his book *Witchcraft at Salem* Professor Chadwick Hanson observes, "Probably the commonest of such [fertility] gods has been the deified sun, but the next commonest was the deified herd animal, the cow, or more often [because of his reputation for lechery] the goat. Half human and half bestial, with horns and cloven hooves, he appeared as Dionysus or Bacchus, the chief fertility god of the classical world, and was also to be found in the pantheons of northern Europe. Apparently the early Christians thought him the most abominable of all the pagan deities; they gave his attributes, his horns and cloven hooves, to the Devil, adding to those the wings of the fallen angel."

The differences between the goat as fertility god and the goat as Devil or evil spirit sprang from the different attitudes of pagans and early Christians toward sex.

Aside from his identification with the serpent and the dragon, the Bible offers no clear description of the Devil. The goatlike Devil seems to have been born first in the visions of the desert fathers, a group of early Christian zealots who fled to the deserts of Egypt during the third and fourth centuries in order to escape the temptations of the flesh. But even in the solitude of the desert these holy hermits were tormented. They said it was demons that attacked them. A modern psychiatrist might explain their torments as sexual fantasies. A figure that recurred frequently in their visions was a half-goat, half-man creature reminiscent of the god Pan or the satyrs of classical mythology. These pagan symbols of sexuality would have been familiar to the early Christians, particularly those in Egypt, which had long been under Roman domination and was heavily influenced by Greek culture. Since early Christianity was profoundly antisexual it is hardly surprising that the archfiend himself would be given the shape of the most familiar symbol of pagan sexuality.

Some modern students of witchcraft claim that the witches really did worship a goat god—not the Devil, who is a Judeo-Christian creation, but rather an ancient horned deity. Other scholars believe

The Devil as a goat. Based on a drawing of the nineteenth-century French occultist Eliphas Levi.

that the witch-hunters simply assumed that witches worshiped the Devil, horns, hooves, and all, and that many of those accused of witchcraft were forced to confess to dealings with such a creature.

However the goat got its reputation as a symbol of the Devil or as the Devil himself, it is the animal most commonly pictured and described in connection with witchcraft ceremonies. In the *Encyclopedia of Witchcraft and Demonology*, Rossell Hope Robbins quotes a typical confession made by an accused witch in 1594. The suspect's lover took her to a sabbat on the eve of St. John the Baptist's Day (June 24). He made a magic circle and invoked a large black goat, two women, and a man dressed like a priest. When the man told the Devil-goat that the girl wished to become his subject:

> The goat ordered her to make the sign of the cross with her left hand, and all present to venerate him. At which all kissed him under the tail. Those present lit candles they were holding from a black candle burning between the goat's horns and dropped money in an offertory bowl.

A large number of supernatural associations have been attached to birds, though they do not hold nearly so fearful a place in the pantheon of evil as the snake, the cat, and the goat. Most often birds are regarded as omens of evil, rather than agents of the Devil or the Devil incarnate. According to Hans Holzer, it was believed that when all the hawks left the site of the old Habsburg castle, that would be a sign that the curse on the Habsburg family had ended.

Even today some people will still say that a bird tapping at a window or a bird flying into a room is a sure sign that someone in the house will die within a year. The late nineteenth-century occultist Abbé Boullan was terrified one night when he thought that he heard a "black bird of death" cry out. This, he said, was a sign that his enemies had invoked a magical spell that would cause his death. As a matter of fact, Boullan did die the very next day.

The crow, because it is black and is often a carrion eater, has a particularly sinister reputation. The list of crow superstitions is practically endless, but most amount to the same idea: The presence of crows, particularly crows doing something unusual, is a sign of impending doom. It was said that several crows were seen fluttering about the head of the Roman statesman Cicero shortly before he was murdered.

Even those who count themselves as resolutely rational and immune to superstitious fears can occasionally be shaken by the appearance of one of these reputed omens of doom. Some years ago my wife and I were on a driving vacation in Maine. At the time there was a popular book that was supposed to be the true story of a couple that had been driving down a road in Maine when they were stopped by strange creatures and taken aboard a flying saucer for several hours. Since we were in the area where this "kidnapping" was reported to have taken place, we decided to take a look.

I didn't believe in flying saucers and thought the whole story was foolish, and I still do. But as we slowly drove down the lonely road toward the spot where the other couple reported being stopped and taken to the flying saucer, I noticed that a crow was following the car. There were plenty of crows around, so the mere sight of one wasn't unusual. But this crow wasn't just flying around; it seemed to be deliberately keeping within a few feet of the car. I tried to ignore it, but kept glancing into the rearview mirror every few seconds to see if it was still there. It was, and it began to make me nervous. I became acutely conscious of the fact that the road ran through a forest and that we had not passed another car for quite a while. I began to think that if something happened no one would know about it for a long time. After two or three miles, the crow veered

An evil spirit in the form of a black bird whispering into the ear of a magician. From an eleventh-century French manuscript.

off and disappeared among the trees. I don't mind saying that I was greatly relieved to see it go.

The presence of the crow was just a coincidence, I'm sure of that now. It seemed spooky at the time because we were on a rather spooky quest. The rest of the drive was uneventful, and we never were able to locate the exact spot where the saucer was supposed to have landed. But for a few moments, I was not as sure as Sherlock Holmes had been in the case of *The Hound of the Baskervilles* that there was a natural explanation for the strange event.

III - ACCURSED PLACES

I am the way to the city of woe . . .
Abandon hope all ye who enter here.
    —*Dante*, The Divine Comedy

MYTHOLOGY AND LITERATURE are replete with tales of places "from which no man has ever returned alive." Popular fable holds that the tomb of the pharaoh Tutankhamen was cursed and that those who defiled the tomb were struck dead. Yet one need not go to fiction, ancient myths, or the imaginative fabrications of enthusiastic newspaper reporters to find a good story of a place that seems to be under a curse. Currently one of the best "real" mystery stories going concerns a place which in an earlier age would have been called accursed. Because this story is so well documented, it gives us an unparalled close-up look at how curse legends might get started and why they are often so widely believed.

There is a part of the South Atlantic known as the Bermuda Triangle. The area has also been called the Devil's Triangle, the Hoodoo Sea, and a lot of other things. Many insist that it is not triangular in shape at all. The boundaries of the region are ill defined, with different authors disagreeing about its size and shape. But for our purposes we will call the area the Bermuda Triangle and say that it is a triangular patch of sea with one point at the island of Bermuda, a second at Puerto Rico, and the third at the southern tip of Florida. Within this area some very strange things have happened.

There is no exact point in time from which we can date the "curse" of the Bermuda Triangle. There is no ancient legend of the Carib Indians which holds that all the canoes that ventured into the region were pulled under by angry sea demons. The legend is recent as such things go. It began when a very mysterious disappearance took place in 1945. Looking back in time people discovered that other strange disappearances had taken place in the same general area. And from time to time since 1945 more mysterious disappearances have been linked to the Bermuda Triangle.

The incident that first set off speculation that there might be something wrong with this bit of the South Atlantic took place on the afternoon of December 5, 1945. A group of five TBF Avenger torpedo bombers took off on a routine training mission from the United States Naval Air Station at Fort Lauderdale, Florida, at 2:10 P.M. Records at the Air Station called the mission Flight 19. The leader of the group was a qualified flight instructor, and the other four members all had several hundred hours of flying time and were experienced with the Avenger type of aircraft. There were light rain showers in the area, but the weather was not considered dangerous or unusual. It was a perfectly ordinary, completely routine training flight, and when the planes took off that afternoon there wasn't a hint of trouble.

The first indication that anything was amiss came at about four o'clock when a radio message, apparently between the leader of the flight and one of the other pilots, was picked up by the base radio operators at Fort Lauderdale. The message indicated that the planes were having trouble with their compasses and that the pilots did not know where they were. A short time later another message from the patrol commander was overheard. In it he relinquished his

Five TBF Avenger torpedo bombers similar to those which disappeared over the Bermuda Triangle on December 5, 1945.

command to another pilot for no apparent reason. The new commander was heard to say, "We can't tell where we are. . . . Everything is . . . can't make out anything . . . . We think we may be about 225 miles northeast of the base." There were a few more inaudible words overheard by the men at the base, then clearly, "Looks like we are . . ." And that was it. Flight 19 was never seen or heard from again, nor was a single bit of wreckage or any other trace of the five planes ever found.

The official Navy report on the incident says dryly, "It is assumed that they crashed at sea, possibly after running out of gas. It is known that the fuel carried by the aircraft would have been completely exhausted by 8 P.M. It is also possible that some unexplained and unforeseen development of weather conditions may have intervened, although there is no evidence of freak storms in the area at the time."

The mystery of the "Lost Patrol," as some writers have dubbed it, was compounded almost immediately during the extensive air and sea search that was mounted following the disappearance. A large Martin Mariner flying boat took off and headed toward the spot where the five Avengers were believed to have disappeared. The Martin Mariner had a specially reinforced hull for making sea landings under rough conditions, and it carried full rescue equipment. Ten minutes after taking off the Martin Mariner radioed a routine position check. That was the last radio message ever received from the plane, for it too disappeared.

The disappearance of the Martin Mariner is not as mysterious as that of the five Avengers because there is at least some indication of what its fate might have been. A merchant ship reported seeing a "burst of flame, apparently an explosion" and some time later passing through an oil slick at the spot where the plane was presumed missing. No such evidence was found in connection with Flight 19.

These back-to-back disappearances started people thinking. Had there been similar cases in the area? Yes, there had, plenty of them. The first that we know of was in 1866. In March of that year the Swedish bark *Lotta*, out of Goteborg and bound for Havana, vanished somewhere in the Bermuda Triangle region. Two years later the Spanish merchantman *Viego* sailed into the Triangle and was never heard from again. In 1880 the British training frigate *Atalanta* left Bermuda and disappeared, and in 1884 it was the Italian schooner *Miramon* that sailed into oblivion in the South Atlantic.

All of these disappearances took place in the days of wooden ships, when putting out to sea was a far more dangerous undertaking than it is today. Uncounted thousands of wooden ships sailed out into the ocean never to be heard from again. As often as not no trace of the ships was ever found, and the fact that a number of them had disappeared within a particular area was not necessarily a cause for surprise or alarm. It wasn't until 1918 that something happened to cause people to take notice.

On March 4 of that year the USS *Cyclops*, a huge tanker loaded with manganese ore being shipped from Brazil to Baltimore, Maryland, stopped at the island of Barbados to take on coal. The ship departed the next day, steamed off into the Bermuda Triangle, and vanished. A total of 309 officers, crewmen, and passengers were lost with the *Cyclops*.

On April 14 the Navy Department announced the *Cyclops* was missing and launched an intensive air and sea search. The ship wasn't found, nor was an oil slick or any wreckage that might give a clue to its fate. On August 30 the Navy gave up its search, concluded that the *Cyclops* was lost for good, and tried to figure out what had happened.

In 1918 the United States was at war with Germany and the most obvious explanation for the disappearance was that the ship with its valuable cargo was sunk by a torpedo from a German U-boat. Yet the *Cyclops* carried a radio and made no report of an attack. Almost certainly the ship would have had time to radio a distress signal. In addition the records of the German Admiralty found after the war indicate there were no U-boats operating in the vicinity at the time. Nor is there any indication that the ship struck a mine, for the lanes in which the *Cyclops* was operating were continually checked for mines. Besides, mine explosions usually leave an abundance of wreckage.

Dozens of other more or less plausible theories have been put forth over the years to account for the tanker's disappearance. None has been very satisfactory. The Navy itself, which dislikes sensational conclusions and has no desire to arouse anyone's fears about the Bermuda Triangle, has nonetheless concluded, "The disappearance of this ship has been one of the most baffling mysteries in the annals of the Navy, all attempts to locate her having proved unsuccessful. Many theories have been advanced, but none that satisfactorily accounts for her disappearance."

While the disappearance of the *Cyclops* must be considered the most mysterious of the ship disappearances within the Bermuda Triangle because the ship involved was the largest and the case most carefully investigated, there were plenty of other ships that followed her into limbo and added to the impression that there is something distinctly "wrong" with the area.

In January, 1925, the American freighter *Cotopaxi* vanished while en route from Charleston, South Carolina, to Havana. Fourteen months later it was the turn of the tramp steamer *Sudoffco* bound for Puerto Rico. A Norwegian ship *Stavanger* was the next to go in October of 1931. And then it was the American freighter *Sandra* that put out from Savannah, Georgia, in June 1950 and was last seen off St. Augustine, Florida. The tanker *Marine Sulpher Queen* disappeared somewhere near Key West in February, 1963. A single life jacket was found floating near the spot from which her last radio message was received.

And it isn't just ships that have vanished. Airplane disappearances have been even more disquieting. The investigators had barely closed their books on the disappearance of Flight 19 when a number of other airplanes were apparently plucked right out of the sky over the Bermuda Triangle. The *Star Tiger* was an American-owned, British-built four-engined Tudor, bound for Jamaica via Bermuda on the night of January 29, 1948. When about four hundred miles northeast of Bermuda, the pilot radioed, "Arriving on schedule." The *Star Tiger* never arrived, and searchers were not able to find so much as a scrap of wreckage.

The British grounded all Tudor IV aircraft pending an investigation. The board of inquiry concluded that the aircraft itself was sound. The final report stated, "What happened will never be known and the aircraft's fate must remain an unsolved mystery."

Since no structural or engine defects could be found the Tudor aircraft were allowed to fly again. Then almost exactly one year after the disappearance of the *Star Tiger* another four-engined Tudor, the *Star Ariel*, vanished in the same area. The plane had taken off from Bermuda on the morning of January 17, 1949. It carried twenty passengers and crew. About half an hour after becoming airborne the pilot radioed, "All's well." That was the only message ever received from the *Star Ariel*. Another board of inquiry was convened, but again no conclusion could be reached. "Through lack of evidence due to no wreckage having been found the cause [of the disappearance] is unknown," the report stated.

In late December of the same year a group of vacationers were returning home from Puerto Rico to Florida aboard a chartered DC-3. The weather was excellent and the passengers were all singing Christmas carols. The captain reported being within sight of land and only fifty miles from Miami. The landing instructions were radioed back, but whether the captain received them or not is unknown for the captain never responded and the plane never landed. It too had disappeared. Bits of wreckage were found in the area where the plane was presumed to have gone down but could never be positively identified.

In 1963 two American stratojet tankers went down at the same time, some three hundred miles west of Bermuda. And there have been more, but the roll call becomes depressingly monotonous.

The raw statistics of the list of "victims" of the Bermuda Triangle is impressive, and just reading the list can be frightening, particularly if one is planning a vacation in Bermuda. However, not all of the cases mentioned are equally mysterious. Were it not for the two most spectacular disappearances, that of the *Cyclops* and particularly that of the five planes of Flight 19, there would be no aura of mystery or terror attached to the Bermuda Triangle. Ships sink and planes crash for a variety of reasons. Radio equipment fails, and wreckage is not found. The phrase "disappeared without a trace" does not automatically raise the fear that some kind of supernatural agency is at work.

As in the case of family curses, statistics should tell the story. It would be nice if we could compare the percentage of planes and ships that have disappeared in the Bermuda Triangle in the past hundred years with the percentage of planes and ships that have disappeared in other areas during the same period of time. Of course, allowances would have to be made for differing weather conditions and other potentially dangerous factors. Then we might see if the Bermuda Triangle or any other area of the world had a significantly higher percentage of disappearances. Unfortunately, despite millions of words that have already been written on the Bermuda Triangle, no such analysis has ever been attempted, and for a very good reason. The sheer mechanics of collecting the data for an analysis is staggering. Besides, there are so many factors which might influence the final result; for example, the exact dimensions of the Bermuda Triangle have never been agreed upon. All that we can really say is that we have an impression that a significantly large number of planes and ships have disappeared mysteriously within the confines of the Bermuda Triangle.

The Bermuda Triangle is by no means the only spot in the world where strange disappearances are reputed to take place with alarming regularity. Another such place is the "Devil's Sea," a small portion of the Pacific between the island of Iwo Jima and Marcus Island southwest of Japan. Unlike the Bermuda Triangle, whose sinister reputation is of recent origin, the bad reputation of the Devil's Sea goes back for centuries among Japanese sailors and fishermen. They described it as an area infested with demons and evil spirits. In fact, the Devil's Sea is a region of underwater volcanoes. This could explain its associations with evil among uneducated fishermen, but cannot explain the numerous disappearances that have taken place within its confines.

For a long time Japanese naval authorities took little notice of the Devil's Sea. The craft that disappeared there were small fishing vessels. Boats of this type are inherently unstable and often barely seaworthy. They can disappear without a trace for many reasons. But starting in the 1950s much bigger ships began to vanish and Japanese naval authorities became concerned. They now regard the Devil's Sea as a "danger zone," though no one is able to explain exactly what the danger is.

A number of other danger zones are associated with unexplained disappearances of one sort or another. How many there are and where they are located depends upon which author one consults.

The Bermuda Triangle gives us a good case study of how a curse story gets started. Interest in the mysterious disappearances began right after the incident of Flight 19 in 1945. But the public didn't really become Bermuda Triangle conscious until the mid-1960s, when a couple of writers began putting all the disappearances together in popular articles. At that point someone coined the name "Bermuda Triangle."

Suddenly what had been a string of strange, but apparently unconnected tragedies were lumped together and given an identifiable title. The mystery which had been attached to each individual case had been fused into the much larger mystery of the place itself. In the latter half of the twentieth century we have created for ourselves a legend of an accursed place as strong as that which medieval peasants attached to gloomy forests or ruined castles.

The late Ivan Sanderson, who liked to see the world being filled with all sorts of weird mysteries for which he could concoct bizarre explanations, wrote extensively on the subject of the Bermuda

Triangle. In his book *Invisible Residents* he said, "After we published our article in *Argosy* magazine on the subject of vortices [Sanderson's explanation for the disappearing planes and ships] we began to receive an ever-increasing flood of letters from terrified tourists and other travelers and potential travelers asking whether it was safe to take a trip to Bermuda. One began to feel sorry for the air and shipping lines, let alone the Bermudan trade and tourist bureaus. As a result, we went to considerable trouble to track down some rumors to the effect that military planes and surface vessels, and commercial airlines, had received instructions not to fly or boat over the area originally designated the 'Bermuda Triangle.'"

Any such rumors, as Sanderson clearly stated, were utter nonsense. The air and sea lanes through the Bermuda Triangle are among the busiest in the world. Millions have passed through this deadly zone unharmed, and often blissfully unaware of where they were. Yet I have known several perfectly intelligent and otherwise reasonable people who expressed great fear about embarking on trips that would carry them through the Bermuda Triangle. Although they all returned from the experience unharmed none of them was particularly anxious to take a similar trip again.

The most reasonable attitude to adopt toward the Bermuda Triangle is that the disappearances that have taken place within it are not connected. They appear mysterious only because we don't know all the facts, and if we did we could undoubtedly find natural explanations for all of them.

But such a reasonable attitude is also profoundly unsatisfying. Many of us secretly suspect and hope that there is something unearthly and deadly about the place. It is not that we are cold-blooded and actually enjoy the spectacle of sailors and airmen vanishing. But a plane crash or a ship sinking is essentially a meaningless tragedy. The idea that the planes and ships succumbed to some sort of unearthly force gives the tragedies a meaning of sorts. As with family curses, the stories are kept alive by our psychological unwillingness to see a universe ruled by blind chance. Then, too, a plane crash, tragic as it may be, is also commonplace. An accursed zone makes the whole thing more exciting; it gives us a brush with the thrilling world of the supernatural.

So let's leave aside the most probable explanation for the moment and look at some of the other explanations that have been advanced for the Bermuda Triangle. In his book *This Baffling World* reporter John Godwin concludes a chapter on the Bermuda Triangle with a question: "Did the lost airplanes and lost ships encounter phenomena unknown to today's science? Do the laws of nature still contain a few paragraphs not covered in our textbooks?"

Those who try to explain the Bermuda Triangle often speak of a "vortex." In common usage a vortex is a whirling mass of fluid, the best-known example being a whirlpool. Just what the word is supposed to mean when applied to the Bermuda Triangle is not at all clear. But it does project the image of the planes and ships being sucked up or down by some sort of strange whirling of air or water.

Another term that pops up often is "time warp." The image here is of the ships and planes going off through a break in the normal time continuum. The time warp idea was invented by writers of science fiction. It is a convenient plot device and has been used so often that some people believe that there is such a thing, but as far as we know there is not.

In our modern age it is no longer quite fashionable to think about regions haunted by evil spirits or protected by angry gods who are ready to snatch up those who violate its boundaries. The modern equivalents of such beliefs hold that the missing ships and planes have been "kidnapped" by extraterrestrials who come to earth in flying saucers, or by ultraterrestrials who live beneath the sea or in some other "dimension." What purpose such beings might have in snatching ships and planes from the Bermuda Triangle or anywhere else is unknown.

There are, of course, numerous tales of cursed and jinxed houses, castles, caves, mountains, and what have you. But none of these tales holds up very well in the modern world, and certainly none of them can match the tales of cursed ships. When it comes to inexplicable runs of bad luck and genuinely mysterious tragedies, the sea has it all over the land.

As we already pointed out, in the days of wooden sailing ships seafaring was an extremely dangerous business. The ships were small and fragile when compared with the enormity and potential violence of the sea. Because of the dangers and uncertainties of their occupation sailors were an exceptionally superstitious group. They had dozens of little rituals aimed at improving their chances of surviving a hazardous voyage. Any ship on which things appeared to go persistently wrong might get the reputation of being a jinxed or hard-luck ship, and sailors would avoid serving on it if at all possible.

Of all the jinxed or cursed ships that have ever sailed, none deserves its reputation more fully than does the *Mary Celeste*. The ship was a 282-ton British brigantine built in Canada in the mid-nineteenth century and originally christened the *Amazon*. Bad luck attended her even before her bow touched seawater. The first man appointed to be her skipper died before the ship was launched. On her maiden voyage she was badly damaged, and while she was being repaired a fire broke out on her. As a result of these mishaps her second skipper was fired. It was under her third captain that the *Amazon* finally made a crossing of the Atlantic—and ran into another ship in the Straits of Dover. With time out for repairs and with a new skipper she returned to Canada in 1867 and promptly ran aground on Cape Breton Island.

After the ship was salvaged she wound up in the hands of an

American named James Winchester. Winchester had her repaired, refitted, and renamed the *Mary Celeste*.

The new master and part-owner of the *Mary Celeste* was Massachusetts born Benjamin Spooner Briggs, and a more trust-worthy and responsible ship's captain was not to be found. At thirty-eight Briggs was already an experienced seaman who had captained three other ships before he took over the *Mary Celeste*. Briggs was a flinty and puritanical New Englander who spoke only when necessary, drank not at all, and subjected his crew to daily Bible readings, though he could never quite bring himself to read the word "damn" aloud.

If Briggs had some trouble in recruiting a crew for a ship with such a bad reputation we know nothing of it. He was well pleased with the crew he got and said of them, "They are all good and willing fellows, but I have yet to find out how smart they are." On his first voyage Captain Briggs planned to take along his wife and

Capt. Benjamin Spooner Briggs, master of the Mary Celeste.

Capt. David Reed Morehouse, master of the Dei Gratia.

baby daughter. Despite the oft repeated superstition that women aboard a ship brought bad luck, captains often took their families on long voyages.

Early in November 1872 the *Mary Celeste* was in New York Harbor being loaded with a cargo of commercial alcohol. Her destination was Genoa, Italy. Nearby was the brigantine *Dei Gratia*, scheduled to leave at about the same time bound for Gibraltar. Captain Briggs was an old friend of the *Dei Gratia*'s skipper, David Reed Morehouse, and their families dined together two days before the *Mary Celeste* departed on November 5. The two ships were to meet again in mid-ocean a month later, in one of the strangest encounters in naval history.

On December 4, 1872, when about six hundred miles off the coast of Portugal, Captain Morehouse was informed that another brigantine, with part of her sails gone, was drifting in the vicinity. As the

The Dei Gratia *encounters the abandoned* Mary Celeste *on December 4, 1872.*

Dei Gratia drew closer the captain recognized the drifter as the *Mary Celeste.*

Through his glass Captain Morehouse saw that there was no one at the wheel, indeed no one on deck at all. He immediately ordered a boarding party. A thorough search of the *Mary Celeste* determined that there was not a soul on board, living or dead. Captain Briggs, his family, and the entire crew had disappeared.

Abandoned ships drifting in mid-ocean are an uncommon, but not an unknown phenomenon. A ship might be attacked by pirates, its crew slaughtered or carried off, and the ship left to drift. A fire or severe storm might damage a ship so badly that its crew felt their chances were better in the lifeboats. Even a mutiny might empty a ship if the mutineers first disposed of their officers and then panicked and tried to escape the scene of their crime in small boats. But there was no sign of violence or extensive damage aboard the *Mary Celeste.* There was no obvious reason why the ship should have been abandoned. She was battered from drifting in the ocean, but completely seaworthy, and there was an ample supply of food on board.

The crew had apparently left in the yawl, a small boat carried by the larger ship. There was every indication that they had left in a hurry. All their personal possessions were still on board. The tales of plates still being set on the table and a fire still burning in the galley are exaggerations, but the truth is hardly less surprising.

The last entry in the ship's log was dated November 24, ten days before the drifter was sighted by the *Dei Gratia.* The ship was found several hundred miles from the last position written in the log. On routine voyages, however, log entries were not made every day unless something unusual occurred, so the *Celeste* may not have drifted as far or as long as the log entry indicated. The log gave no clue to the fate that had befallen captain and crew. The final entry simply read, "about 110 miles due west of the island of Santa Maria in the Azores."

Despite the shock of finding his friend's ship abandoned under the strangest possible circumstances, Captain Morehouse must also have counted the incident as a stroke of extreme good fortune, for under the laws of salvage he could lay claim to the *Mary Celeste* and her valuable cargo. He put a few of his men aboard and they were able to sail the *Celeste* to Gibraltar without incident, further proof of the vessel's seaworthiness.

After the ship reached Gibraltar there was an investigation and a host of legal problems. Morehouse was able to collect only a portion of his reward. The ship itself was finally returned to its owner, James Winchester, who promptly sold it for whatever he could get.

For the rest of her career the *Mary Celeste*'s reputation as a jinx ship remained intact with a series of mishaps, minor accidents, fires, and the untimely deaths of her masters. Her career came to an end in 1884 when she wound up in the possession of an unscrupulous owner named Gilman C. Parker. Parker decided to ditch the *Celeste* for the insurance she carried. Ship and cargo had been insured for $27,000, far above their true worth. Parker had the ship run aground on a reef in Haiti and then set fire to her. Even in this final act the *Celeste* served up bad luck for her owner.

The insurance company was suspicious of Parker's claims, and its investigators turned up some crew members who were willing to tell what really happened on the *Mary Celeste*'s last voyage. Parker and three of his officers barely escaped conviction for deliberately destroying their ship—the crime of barratry and a hanging offense. Parker never collected a penny on his claim and died in poverty and disrepute a few months later.

The story of the *Mary Celeste* follows the same pattern as many other curse stories. There is a single spectacular incident which focuses attention on the case. After that investigators discover a number of more or less minor mishaps which may or may not be related to the main disaster that first brought notoriety.

Aside from the disappearance of all aboard in 1872 the rest of the bad luck suffered by the *Mary Celeste*, her owners, and crew might simply be a string of unhappy coincidences. There were doubtless hundreds, even thousands of ships which had piled up equally dismal records without becoming legendary. However, the disappearance of Captain Briggs and his family and crew is another matter altogether. Other ships had been found adrift, but there was always at least some hint of what had happened. Such was not the case with the *Celeste*.

Captain Morehouse and his men had no theories about what had happened, or if they had they kept quiet about them. The first man to offer an explanation for the mystery was the advocate general of Gibraltar, where the *Dei Gratia*'s crew had sailed the *Mary Celeste*. The advocate general was suspicious because of the close connection between the skipper of the *Celeste* and the skipper of the ship that found her. He intimated that Captain Morehouse, upon learning of the *Celeste*'s valuable cargo, overtook her in mid-ocean and had her captain and crew murdered and thrown overboard so that he could claim salvage rights. The difficulty with this theory was that a mass murder would surely have left some signs of struggle aboard the *Celeste*. There were none, nor would any of the *Dei Gratia*'s crew confess to such a crime.

Another possible explanation offered by the advocate general was that the crew of the *Celeste* had "got at" the alcohol she was carrying, murdered the captain, his family, and the mate in a drunken fury, and then taken off in the small boat. But again, the absence of any signs of struggle made the theory hard to swallow. Besides, commercial alcohol would not have made the crew drunk; it would have killed them. The court of inquiry at Gibraltar rejected both theories. As to what did happen to the *Mary Celeste*, the court offered no explanation.

In the more than a century that has followed the disappearance of the *Mary Celeste*'s crew every conceivable bit of information about the case has been examined and reexamined. There is probably no incident in naval history that has gotten such a thorough going-over. Since all the eyewitnesses to the disappearance have themselves disappeared and the ship is no longer available for study, it is highly doubtful if any new information will turn up. I'm not going to offer any theories about what happened. It is a mystery, and we must be content to leave it at that. But a look at some of the theories that have been advanced in the past century gives us a fairly good idea of how modern man confronts and tries to explain a brush with the unknown.

The *Mary Celeste*'s owner, James Winchester, was a practical, down-to-earth fellow and no believer in curses. He proposed the most reasonable, and one of the dullest, explanations for the mystery. The cargo, Winchester pointed out, was crude alcohol. The vapors escaping from one of the barrels might have caused a minor explosion, not enough to do any structural damage that would have been detected after the ship was found, but enough to frighten captain and crew badly. Since Captain Briggs had no experience with such a cargo he might have feared that his ship was about to blow up. His anxiety would surely have been increased by the presence of his wife and baby. Captain and crew would have piled into the yawl, though Briggs would have had enough presence of mind to take the sextant and navigation books, which were missing when the *Celeste* was found. This abandonment would have taken place several hundred miles from the nearest land. Briggs doubtless hoped to get back aboard the *Celeste* if and when the danger passed. However, the small yawl could easily have been swamped by a wave and the empty *Mary Celeste* left to drift and become a legend of the sea.

Another fairly reasonable explanation that has been put forth recently is that the ship's company ate bread contaminated with the fungus ergot. This fungus can damage the central nervous system. The fungus could literally have driven captain and crew mad and caused them to irrationally abandon ship.

A host of objections can be raised to either explanation, and they have never had large followings among mystery-of-the-sea buffs, possibly because they are not very exciting. Actually, the *Mary Celeste* mystery didn't attract much attention for years. It was only when writers began coming up with sensational "solutions" to the mystery that it captured the public's imagination.

Around the turn of the century sea monster theories were popular. These held that a monster had surfaced near the ship and picked off the occupants of the *Mary Celeste* with its tentacles, or alternately that it had frightened them into abandoning ship. Just why, in the presence of a sea monster, the crew would abandon a large ship, however unsafe they felt it to be, for a smaller one is not explained. But then the theory itself isn't very good; it is just popular.

Current explanations tend to lean toward the hypothesis that the *Mary Celeste* was the victim of some sort of mysterious force which took the humans aboard but left the ship intact. It has been rumored that flying saucers were responsible. Currently a number of writers have linked the mystery of the *Mary Celeste* with those of the Bermuda Triangle and dozens of other unexplained disappearances. All of this is supposed to prove that we are being watched or controlled by alien powers.

Theories like these are not based so much on fact as they are on fear—fear of the unknown. For all our science and education we aren't much different from our ancestors who were afraid to go into the darkest part of the forest because it was rumored to be cursed.

IV - CURSES OF WANDERERS AND GHOSTS

Like one, that on a lonesome road
Doth walk in fear and dread,
And having once turned round walks on,
And turns no more his head;
Because he knows, a frightful fiend
Doth close behind him tread.
—Samuel Taylor Coleridge

IN SAMUEL TAYLOR COLERIDGE'S POEM "The Rime of the Ancient Mariner," the narrator is a figure who has been cursed for killing an albatross. The albatross is considered by sailors to be a bird of good fortune, and in killing one the ancient mariner broke some law of nature or God. Among his punishments the mariner is forced to wander from place to place and tell his story to everyone who will listen.

The idea that a man accursed must wander for years, perhaps for all eternity, is an ancient one. In the Greek legends Oedipus became a wanderer for his crimes, and Orestes was driven to wander by the Furies.

The curse of wandering has an obvious historical foundation. In ancient times individuals were often condemned to banishment and driven from their home villages or cities for their crimes. Banishment was no light punishment. A wanderer usually found himself

The Ancient Mariner with the albatross hung round his neck.

alone and friendless in the wilderness. You may recall that one of the punishments that God laid upon Cain for the killing of his brother was that "You shall be a vagrant and wander on earth" (Gen. 4:12). Then Cain protested that as a wanderer he could be killed by anyone. Cain's fear was real enough, for in ancient times outsiders were rarely welcomed or even tolerated. Strangers might be killed as a matter of course.

So the curse of wandering has ample historical precedent, and it

is one that would have seemed more terrible to people of past ages
than to men of the modern world. The curse of the wanderer has
brought forth one of the most haunting and persistent legends of all
times, that of the Wandering Jew. The legend has come down to us
in many forms, but basically the tale is the same. Shortly before the
crucifixion, goes the story, there was a Jew living in Jerusalem who
offended Jesus in some way. (The nature of the offense varies from
story to story, but usually the offense seems a rather minor one.) As
a result, however, Jesus decreed that the Jew was to remain upon
earth until He returned, that is until the time of the Second
Coming.

The Wandering Jew. From a nineteenth-century French drawing.

The legend has been around for so long that some people have the impression that the story can be found in the Bible, but this isn't so. Perhaps the seeds of the Wandering Jew legend can be traced to biblical phrases like this one in Mark 16:28. "I tell you this: there are some of those standing here who will not taste death before they have seen the Son of Man coming in his kingdom." Such biblical statements which indicate that Christ would return before all of those who were alive during His time on earth had died had to be interpreted allegorically, or one had to assume that there was at least one individual who had remained alive since the time of Christ.

But relating the legend directly back to the Bible seems more of an afterthought. The tradition that there are certain individuals who have, for one reason or another, attained immortality on this earth was always a popular one in Europe and is not necessarily related to Christian belief at all. It almost certainly goes back to pagan legends and beliefs in which certain heroes attained immortality for their deeds. Even in Christian times such legends were attached to great heroes. King Arthur, Charlemagne, Frederick Barbarossa, and others were all, at one time or another, rumored never to have died, but rather to be sleeping or hiding in some secret place, awaiting the proper moment to return. Conquered people often consoled themselves with sleeping-hero legends and kept their own hopes alive with the fantasy that one of their great leaders of the past would return to carry them out of bondage. From time to time impostors or madmen claiming to be one of these sleeping heroes were able to gather considerable followings.

There is an additional basis for the legend of the Wandering Jew. It developed during the Middle Ages, often a time of ferocious anti-Semitism. This tale of the Jew who had insulted Jesus and was cursed for eternity became a convenient stick with which medieval Christians could beat the Jews of their day. The Wandering Jew became a symbol for all Jews, who were forced by persecution to move from place to place, and a justification for the persecution.

Whatever the reason or reasons behind the origin of this tale, it became an astonishingly persistent and persuasive one. Starting in about the thirteenth century, there were dozens of accounts, often written by learned and eminent men, which related how the teller or someone that he had talked to had seen the Wandering Jew in the flesh.

This early seventeenth-century account, quoted by Sabine Baring-Gould in the book *Curious Myths of the Middle Ages*, is fairly typical of the vast literature concerning the appearance of the Wandering Jew:

> Paul von Eitzen, doctor of the Holy Scriptures and Bishop of Schleswig, related as true for some years past that when he was young, having studied at Württemberg, he returned home to his parents in Hamburg in the winter of the year 1547, and that on the following Sunday, in church, he observed a tall man with his hair hanging over his shoulders, standing barefoot during the sermon, over against the pulpit, listening with deepest attention to the discourse, and whenever the name of Jesus was mentioned, bowing himself profoundly and humbly with sighs and beating of the breast. He had no other clothing in the bitter cold of the winter, except a pair of hose which were in tatters about his feet, and a coat with a girdle which reached to his feet; and his general appearance was that of a man of fifty years. And many people, some of high degree and title, have seen this same man in England, France, Italy, Hungary, Persia, Spain, Poland, Moscow, Lapland, Sweden, Denmark, Scotland and other places.

When the doctor asked the tall stranger who he was, the stranger replied that his name was Ahasverus, a shoemaker, and that he had lived in Jerusalem at the time of Christ. The Jew said that he had believed Jesus to be a deceiver of the people. When Jesus was carrying the cross past the shoemaker's shop He stopped to rest for a moment. The angry shoemaker told Him to hurry on. Jesus did move on but said, "I shall stand and rest, but thou shalt go till the last day." Certainly this was a curse, though medieval Christians would probably not have labeled it as such. In any case the shoemaker suddenly found that he was no longer able to stand still. He followed Jesus and witnessed the crucifixion, and then he was compelled to continue moving from place to place, never aging, but never able to rest for long. In this account the Wandering Jew expressed his great desire for death in order to be released from his wandering. Other accounts have the Jew growing older and older until he reaches the age of about one hundred, then suddenly and miraculously being made young again.

It is difficult to know what to make of such a story. The most probable (and disappointing) explanation is that it was simply made up. But another probable explanation is that Doctor von Eitzen really did meet someone who said that he was the Wandering Jew. Of course, not the real immortal Wandering Jew himself, but an impostor or a madman claiming that he was that cursed individual. As late as the mid-nineteenth century ragged figures would wander into various European cities and towns proclaiming that they were the Wandering Jew. Usually these impostures were quickly exposed and the impostor either jailed or ridiculed. But in an age where the legend was more strongly believed, even the most learned and intelligent of men might take the improbable statements of the ragged but grave-looking stranger at face value.

A Swiss version of the legend gives it an even more portentous import. According to that legend one day the Wandering Jew was seen standing on the Matterberg, a hill which is below the Matterhorn. It was said that he had stood on that spot once before, when it was the site of a flourishing city, but that now it was covered only with grass and flowers. According to the Swiss the Wandering Jew will visit the hill once again, on the eve of the Day of Judgment.

A similar and even odder legend concerns the man in the moon. There is a common European folk tradition that the dark markings on the moon are a man carrying a huge bundle of sticks. Personally, I have never seen the resemblance myself, but in Europe the story was once widespread. According to legend the man had been placed on the moon for breaking the Sabbath. The legend can be related back to the Old Testament. In Numbers 15:32–36, there is this story:

> During the time that the Israelites were in the wilderness, a man was found gathering sticks on the Sabbath day. Those who had caught him in the act brought him to Moses and Aaron and all the community, and they kept him in custody, because it was not clearly known what was to be done with him. The Lord said to Moses, "The man must be put to death; he must be stoned by all the community outside the camp." So they took him outside the camp and all stoned him to death, as the Lord commanded Moses.

The man in the moon with his bundle of sticks on his back.

There is no mention of eternal banishment on the moon in the Bible. The Sabbath-breaker was killed quickly and brutally as was the custom in those days. One suspects that in later times people got the idea that a man with a bundle of sticks could be seen on the moon and then went to the Bible in an attempt to explain the phenomenon.

An old German folk tale quoted by Baring-Gould presents the origin of the man-in-the-moon story in a more straightforward manner:

> Ages ago there went one Sunday morning an old man into the wood to hew sticks. He cut a faggot and slung it on a stout staff, cast it over his shoulder, and began to trudge home with his burden. On his way he met a handsome man in Sunday suit, walking toward the Church; this man stopped and asked the faggot-bearer, "Do you know that this is Sunday on earth, when all must rest from their labours?"
>
> "Sunday on earth, or Monday in heaven, it is all one to me!" laughed the wood-cutter.
>
> "Then bear your bundle for ever," answered the stranger; "and as you value not Sunday on earth, yours shall be a perpetual Moon-day in heaven; and you shall stand for eternity in the moon, a warning to all Sabbath-breakers." Thereupon the stranger vanished, and the man was caught up with his staff and his faggots into the moon, where he stands yet.

By the time this German version was set down the tale seems to have become little more than a nursery story, but it is not hard to imagine that at one time the vision of the man in the moon could genuinely terrify potential Sabbath-breakers.

Yet another person cursed to a deathless life of wandering was the Wild Huntsman, who according to European legend can be seen at night in the forest on an everlasting chase because he offended God by saying that he wished to chase the red deer forever. Actually the origin of this particular legend predates Christianity by many centuries. Its history is complex but significant, and it gives us a good example of how a myth changes as it is adopted by different peoples at different times.

The legend seems to have begun in ancient times with pagan cults like those of the wine god Dionysus or the goddess Diana. The initiates of such cults, often women, were said to roam the woods and fields in a wild frenzy. In this state they were likely to tear apart and eat any living thing that they encountered. Unsurprisingly, they were much feared.

The cults themselves were generally limited to the Mediterranean world, but the idea that there were bands which rushed with wild abandon through the woods was carried far beyond the area in

Nineteenth-century conception of the Wild Huntsman.

which the cults themselves existed. Perhaps some Northern European pagans practiced similar rites. From this background arose the idea of the Wild Hunt, a belief that there were individuals who rode out at night with the spirits, often as followers of the goddess Diana (the virgin huntress) or of some local hunting deity. Whether there really was some form of Wild Hunt in the early Middle Ages or the whole thing was a fantasy, we do not know. After the triumph of Christianity, many Christian writers were strongly disinclined to believe in the Wild Hunt. Some church officials actually forbade their flocks to believe in it. Yet the idea of the Wild Hunt lingered on, and gradually Christian skepticism was replaced by Christian fear as legends of the Wild Hunt were merged into ideas about witchcraft. It was from the legend of the Wild Hunt that the idea that witches could fly and gathered nightly in large assemblies first developed.

After the hysterical fear of witchcraft died out ideas about the Wild Hunt changed again. Now, instead of being witches, those who rode through the forests at night were figures to be pitied, not feared, for they had become the individuals cursed to roam the woods forever in an endless chase.

The goddess Diana, thought by some to be the leader of the Wild Hunt and a divinity of the witches.

This legend persists in the most unlikely places. In the 1950s a popular song called "Ghost Riders in The Sky" gave an American Country and Western version of the old Wild Hunt.

More famous than the Wild Huntsman today is the tale concerning the phantom ship often identified as the *Flying Dutchman*. In one version of this tale there is a ship's captain who vowed to sail around Cape Horn whether God willed it or not, and for his blasphemy he was doomed to sail round the Horn forever. Sailors occasionally reported seeing the phantom ship, and it was invariably regarded as an omen of ill luck.

With the legends of the *Flying Dutchman* and the Wild Huntsman we are at the borderline of what is called the ghost story. Actually there is no clear line of demarcation between something like the legend of the Wandering Jew and the thousands upon thousands of ghost stories in which the spirit wanders the earth instead of finding peace in heaven or in the grave.

The belief in the restless and wandering ghost probably goes back to prehistoric times. In many primitive societies there exists a very strong fear that if a body is not buried properly, the spirit of the dead person will not find rest and will come back to haunt or otherwise torment those who failed to arrange the proper burial rites.

In more modern times concern about proper burial is not as obsessive as it was in the past, but the belief that the spirits of the dead might continue to walk and continue to trouble the living persisted, indeed still persists today. Most feared were the spirits of those who had died by suicide or violence. It was assumed that these lives had been cut off before their appointed time. Thus the spirits had unfinished business to perform on the earth. In England until 1823 it was required that a stake be driven through the heart of a suicide victim before the body could be buried. This act, which is connected in popular fiction with vampires, was a means of assuring that the restless spirit of the suicide would stay in the grave where it belonged.

Not only was the ghost in a sense cursed; so too was anyone the ghost happened to encounter. A petition written in England in the late seventeenth century explains the case of a man who believed that his illness was being caused by the ghost of a neighbor who had recently hanged himself. In order to be rid of the troublesome ghost the man employed the services of Robert Tooley, a "doctor and conjurer" of Widdicombe-in-the-Moor, who undertook to remove the curse of the suicide's ghost by magic. This account of the incident is quoted by the British historian Keith Thomas in *Religion and the Decline of Magic.*

> The wife of the said sick man was to get two stout men in the night time with two swords to go to the grave of the man that hanged himself and the one was to stand at the head of the grave and the other at the foot for an hour's time to flourish their swords whilst the said Tooley with a bottle of brandy stood by to conjure the said spirit; which accordingly was performed and done and at which time of the conjuration the doctor told the said wife of the sick person that she would hear a strange noise in and about the house; and also pretended to cure the sick person by putting a grey owl cut into parts and newly killed and bound to the head of the said sick person with a new horse shoe, each hole being filled up with nails; and so the sick person was to wear it next to his skin under his armpit; and about twelve o'clock in the night season she was to go to the house of him that hanged himself and fetch seven motes of straw and he would make a pincase for him to wear under the other arm next to his skin and that would be a present cure.

Tooley charged twenty shillings for his services, a rather consider-able sum in those days. Still the sick man got no better, and he refused to pay. But Tooley, who was apparently a wizard who did not issue a money back guarantee, demanded his payment anyway. He was so persistent that, according to the petition, the sick man and his wife "cannot live in quiet but are forced to shut their door when they see him coming. . . ."

The belief that a troubled spirit is fated to hover about the spot at which he or she was killed remains with us even today. A house in which a suicide or murder has taken place might quickly get the reputation of being haunted, even if there were no reports of ghosts or spirits seen or otherwise perceived there. Such places were simply assumed to be haunted. Many people express a genuine reluctance to stay in a room in which a person has died even a natural death. There is little practical difference between a house that is supposed to be haunted and one that is supposed to be cursed, since it is rarely believed that the appearance of a ghost provides anything other than ill luck.

Nor are houses the only places that have reputations for being haunted; any spot at which a violent death has taken place can easily get such a reputation.

The subject of ghostly curses is far too vast to be covered here, but it does seem appropriate to recount what may well be the most widely told "true" ghost-curse story in modern America.

I first heard it when I was growing up in Chicago, Illinois. It was told to me in all seriousness as a true story. It concerned a man who was driving along a deserted stretch of highway a few miles to the north of the city on a stormy night. The person who told me the story was quite exact about the location, and I was impressed because I had been along the same highway several times. Knowing the location gave me a greater belief in the story's reality.

Much to his surprise the driver in the tale saw a young woman standing along the side of the road, apparently trying to hitch a ride. Though he did not normally like to pick up hitchhikers, the man felt that he simply could not ignore the girl on such a night.

He stopped the car and asked her where she was going. She mentioned an address on the north side of Chicago, and he said that he was going right by and would drop her off. Then the girl said that she was very tired and asked if she might take a nap in the back seat. He agreed and drove on in silence until he reached the address the girl had given him. But when he turned around to tell her that they had arrived, he found that the back seat of his car was empty. The windows had been rolled up because of the rain, the doors were locked, and he had not stopped since he picked up the girl. There was no possible way she could have gotten out of the car. Yet she was gone.

Surprised and quite shaken by the experience, the man decided to ring the doorbell of the address that the girl had given him, despite the lateness of the hour. After a few minutes a middle-aged man in a robe came to the door. The drive apologized profusely for waking him, but explained that something very strange had just happened and that he had to tell someone about it.

As the driver told his story, the man in the robe didn't look surprised or angry; he merely nodded. When the driver finished the recitation the man in the robe said that this was the sixth time the same sort of thing had happened since his daughter was killed in an auto accident at the very spot where the man had picked up the mysterious girl.

As I said, this story was told to me as true, though I'm not sure that I entirely believed it at the time. Since that first experience with the ghostly hitchhiker story, I have heard it at least three other times from different sources. The story is always the same except that different people have placed the story in North Carolina, on a road near St. Louis, Missouri, and in southern California. I have no idea where the story first started. Nor do I know whether it was based upon a real incident or is a modern adaptation of a much older story. But it seems probable that its wide popularity is due primarily to the almost universally held belief that the spirit of a person who has died by violence is fated to return to the spot at which the violence was committed. It is the curse of the eternal wanderer all over again.

V - EVERYDAY CURSES

My name it is Sam Hall, it is Sam Hall.
My name it is Sam Hall, and I hate you one and all.
Yes I hate you one and all, God damn your eyes!
                                        —American folk song

A CURSE is not a wholly evil thing. Curses or the threat of curses have served as means of maintaining the morality of a society. They have provided a measure of power for the powerless, a check on the potential lawbreaker, and in the very least an emotional release for those who feel they have been unjustly wronged.

Take, for example, a dying man. What assurance had he that the provisions of his will would be carried out and that his wife and children would not be preyed upon by the unscrupulous? But so long as the threat of a ghost hung over the living, then the dead man might still provide a measure of security for his family. A seventeenth-century Englishman wrote that ghosts were active "in detecting the murderer, in disposing of their estate, in rebuking injurious executors, in visiting and counselling their wives and children, in forewarning them of such and such courses, and with other matters of like sort."

As Keith Thomas observed, "From the potential criminal's point of view, the role of ghost-beliefs is even more obvious; they served as an extra sanction against crime by holding out the prospect of supernatural detection. Even if a man knew that there would be no witnesses to his evil-doing he still had to face the prospect that his victim might return supernaturally to denounce the crime."

In Shakespeare's play *Macbeth*, the ghost of the murdered Banquo appears silently to rebuke his murderer. This scene would not have been regarded as sheer fantasy by the audience of Shakespeare's time. Why should it have been? They had all heard dozens of apparently true stories in which a ghost had returned to identify or punish his murderer. A penny tract which was sold on the streets of London in 1679 has a title which tells the entire story:

> Strange and Wonderful news from Lincolnshire. Or a Dreadful account of a Most Inhuman and Bloody Murther, committed upon the Body of one Mr. Carter by the Contrivance of his elder Brother, who had hired three more villains to commit the Horrid Fact, and how it was soon found out by the Appearance of a Most Dreadful and Terrible Ghost, sent by Almighty Providence for the Discovery.

It does not matter that the story of Mr. Carter's ghost was probably not "true," or even that the penny tract may well have been entirely fictional rather than error or exaggeration. The point is that the story was presented as fact, and many people accepted it as such. Even the well-educated, who generally did not read penny tracts, would still largely have accepted the avenging-ghost idea as one which was reasonable and supported by centuries of tradition.

A belief in avenging ghosts naturally and inevitably led to a belief in the curse from beyond the grave. The dead man did not actually have to return as a ghost to punish his enemies. A curse uttered by a dying man was believed to be exceptionally effective in setting into motion whatever supernatural forces were necessary to bring disaster to those cursed.

Because of the strength of this belief accounts of curses uttered by dying or condemned men are common. The American folk song "Sam Hall" is just one of a vast body of American murder ballads in which the victim or the condemned curses those who brought about his death. But, like accounts of prophetic last words of great men or deathbed conversions and confessions, such stories must be taken with a large grain of salt. After all, any statement can be attributed to a dead man since he is not around to refute it. Usually these dying curses became known only after some enemy of the dead man suffered a disaster of his own. But still such stories were widely believed and endlessly repeated.

One of these curses of the dying, or in this case the condemned, was that attributed to Jacques de Molay, Grand Master of the Knights Templar. The Templars were a powerful and exceedingly wealthy order of military monks. The order had been started during the time of the Crusades to guard pilgrims on their way to the Holy Land and defend the Christian Kingdom in Palestine.

After the fall of the Crusader's kingdom the Templars managed to retain much of their power and wealth in Europe. Philip IV, King of France, coveted the riches of the order to fill his own depleted coffers. He accused them of a variety of crimes including the practice of magic and heresy. The charges were certainly exaggerated and may have been entirely false. Still the Templars were found guilty, and the punishment meted out against them was unsparingly brutal. Molay and most of the other Templar leaders were tortured and burned at the stake. Molay was executed on March 14, 1314. While standing in the flames he was said to have cursed King Philip, prophesying that the king would die within a year. Philip actually did die in November of that year. According to tradition his death was the result of his being gored by a wild boar. The curse of Jacques de Molay seemed to have been carried out.

One of the reasons that the curse of the Grand Master of the Templars is so well remembered is that it was generally believed that the order was involved in magic and the worship of devils, which would have made them exceptionally adept at cursing.

The centuries of the persecution of witches produced more than their share of tales of curses from the condemned. While the vast majority of the thousands who were executed for witchcraft went to their deaths silently—usually too broken by their previous ordeal to say anything—or protesting their innocence and proclaiming their love of God and Christ, a few exceptionally hardy souls were carried to the stake screaming defiance at their tormentors and threatening them with the wrath of all the demons in hell.

A woman named La Vosin was implicated in some rather unsavory magical goings-on in Paris during the reign of Louis XIV. She was hideously tortured and condemned to be burned alive. The sentence was carried out on February 22, 1680. According to a letter written by one who witnessed the burning of La Vosin, she was forced to the stake "tied and bound with iron. Cursing all the time, she was covered with straw, which five or six times she threw off her, but at last the flames grew fiercer, and she was lost to sight."

But cursing was not the sole province of the dying; nor was it necessary to invoke demons or magic in order to carry off a successful curse. In the Middle Ages many people believed that it was as proper for an unjustly wronged person to curse as it was for him to pray. Biblical accounts like those of the curses of Cain and of Ham and popular legends like that of the Wandering Jew appeared to provide evidence that God punished evil on this earth as well as in heaven, and that it was not always essential to love one's enemies or turn the other cheek.

In the Middle Ages the Church itself claimed the right to pronounce curses. Papal letters often carried an anathema, a formal ecclesiastical curse involving excommunication, on those who disregarded its contents. Priests had the right to curse those who refused to pay their tithes. Church charters and deeds traditionally ended with a strong curse on all who might violate them. Even monastic librarians might attach an anathema to volumes as a guard against thieves and careless borrowers. This is a practice that one suspects many modern librarians would like to see revived.

The full sentence of excommunication by bell, book, and candle might have appeared, to those unfamiliar with theological subtleties, as a curse complete with magical trappings. It was an impressive and terrible ceremony.

On a less august level one Thomas Perne who lived in Cambridgeshire, England, in the fifteenth century was robbed. He reported the theft to his vicar, who published it in church and threatened to curse the thieves if the goods were not immediately restored. In 1521 the Mayor of Lincoln published a formal curse against those who had taken the records and books of the Common Council.

Up until fairly recent times parents were assumed to be invested with at least a measure of divine authority over their children. For a child to seek his parents' blessing for something was no mere act of family politeness. It was a solemn, almost supernatural occasion, the origins of which went back at least as far as the time of the Hebrew patriarchs. Conversely, if a parent had the right to bless, he also had the right to curse his children. "Dread the curse of parents thine. It is a heavy thing," wrote Hugh Rhodes, a fifteenth-century Englishman, and for centuries writers consistently affirmed the power of a parent's curse. "A parent . . . curses his child and God says Amen to it. Hereupon the child is obsessed or strangely handled peradventure perishes," wrote John Gaule in a pamphlet published in

1646. Gaule thought that the parent's curse was "a thing of too common example."

Keith Thomas cites an incident on the day of a wedding in 1655 when one Rachel Dewsall of Herford "pulled up her clothes and kneeled down upon her bare knees and cursed her son and her daughter and wished that they might never prosper." This incident was considered more than a breech of good manners; it was a real and fearful curse.

Says Thomas, "Few can have had the presence of mind of the Marian martyr, Julius Palmer, who after his mother refused her blessing and called down Christ's curse upon him for his heresy, gently reminded her that she had no authority to pronounce God's judgements."

Primarily, though, the curse was a weapon of the poor and the powerless. Lacking any other means of righting or avenging the multiple injuries that they suffered, they turned to God in the belief that He would punish their enemies. Nor was this belief entirely an idle one, for the curse of a poor or wronged man was much to be feared. It is probable that more than once a powerful man hesitated in his oppression of the poor for fear of being cursed.

Thomas continues:

> But it was above all the poor and injured whose curses were believed likely to take effect. The legend of the Beggar's Curse—the fateful malediction upon those who refused alms—enjoyed a continuous currency from the Dark Ages to the nineteenth century. The idea that God would avenge all injuries, and that moral retribution was to be found in this world no less than the next was the justification for the curses and maledictions which were such an enduring feature of sixteenth and seventeenth-century village life.

The power attributed to these curses can be seen in the story of one John Tregoss. At some point during the Middle Ages, Tregoss managed to cheat a widow and her children out of their lands. There followed a long series of financial disasters for the Tregoss family, and in the seventeenth century Thomas Tregoss, a clergyman, had to spend many hours praying for the release of his family from the curse.

Though cursing of this sort was not encouraged by religious authorities, it was not entirely discouraged either. Many common folk felt there was nothing wrong with a good curse so long as they had suffered a genuine injury which had to be avenged, and they called upon God rather than the Devil to carry out the curse. The key was genuine injury. If someone cursed without good cause or tried to curse an innocent person the curse would rebound doubly upon him who uttered it.

These common curses were usually placed with a minimum of ceremony, though the offended person might get down on his or her knees in some public place before witnesses to solemnify the event. The curses tended to be simple and direct in the types of torment that they specified for their victims. "A heavy pox to the ninth generation," "Pox, piles, and a heavy vengeance," and "God's curse and all the plagues of Egypt" were all frequently uttered curses in sixteenth- and seventeenth-century England. Some cursers, however, displayed more ingenuity. In 1673 Jane Smyth cursed a Mrs. Rod of Hertford, "wishing that before she died she might crawl upon the ground like a toad upon all fours." In 1608 Alice Skilling told the local minister and churchwardens that she hoped "the meat and drink they ate might go up and down in their bellies as men go to harrow."

The English, of course, were not the only people who habitually cursed one another. My Russian-Jewish grandmother recounted a curse to me that she said had been common in her youth in the Old

Country. It sticks in my mind precisely because I have never been quite sure what it meant. Translated it is:

"You should grow like an onion, with your head in the sand!"

But neither open cursing nor kneeling was necessary in order to cause harm to befall someone who had angered or wronged you. The simplest, oldest, and most widely accepted method of causing harm was with a withering glance. This was the famous evil eye.

The British antiquarian and student of ancient occultism Sir E. A. Wallis Budge writes in *Amulets and Talismans*: "Of all the things which have driven man in all ages to invent and to use magic, the most potent is the Evil Eye or the Evil Look. And the reason for this is that the various races of men who have peopled the earth for several thousands of years were convinced that certain men and women, certain beasts and reptiles, and even apparently inanimate objects, possess the power of causing by a mere glance of the eye or a look, or by a mere aspect or appearance, injury to their fellow creatures, and to their flocks and herds, and to their crops and orchards, and in fact to any kind of property whatsoever."

Budge asserts that every language, both ancient and modern, contains a word or expression which is the equivalent of "the evil eye." He finds the first mention of the evil eye in the clay tablets of the Sumerians, the oldest known civilization in the world.

It is assumed that the Hebrews too believed in the evil eye. Though there is no direct mention of it in the Old Testament, a number of passages have been interpreted as referring to the evil eye. New Testament references are fairly explicit. In Mark there is talk of evil thoughts and the evil eye. In Matthew there is the phrase, "If thine eye be evil, thy whole body shall be full of darkness."

The thirteenth-century Christian philosopher Thomas Aquinas fully accepted the idea of the evil eye and noted that children were especially vulnerable to the glares of old women. In succeeding

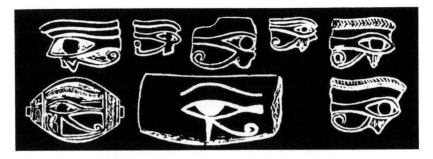

Amulets from North Africa and the Middle East. The design is the traditional ancient Egyptian "eye of Horus." Later peoples adapted this design and used it as a protection from the evil eye.

centuries belief in the evil eye became incorporated into witchcraft beliefs. The fifteenth-century work *Malleus Maleficarum,* compiled by two Dominican Inquisitors, was essentially the bible of witch hunting. In it the authors state "that there are witches who can bewitch their judges by a mere look or glance from their eyes, and publicly boast that they cannot be punished." Another witch-hunter wrote, "Fascination is a power derived from a pact with the Devil, who, when the so-called fascinator looks at another with an evil intent . . . infects with evil the person at whom he looks."

Belief in the evil eye survived the witchcraft hysteria, and possession of the evil eye was credited to some rather surprising individuals, including the poet Lord Byron and two nineteenth-century popes. The popes apparently got the reputation because a great number of cardinals died during their pontificates.

This ancient fear continues to survive today, though now it seems to be primarily a folk belief and is no longer in favor among more sophisticated occultists.

VI - BLACK MAGIC

Fillet of a fenny snake
In the cauldron boil and bake
Eye of newt, and toe of frog
Wool of bat, and tongue of dog
Adder's fork, and blind worm's sting
Lizard's leg, and howlet's wing—
For a charm of powerful trouble,
Like a hell-broth boil and bubble.
                              —Shakespeare

WHEN ONE MENTIONS black magic, one image that comes to mind is that of the three witches in the play *Macbeth*. The scene is among the most widely known in all of Shakespeare's plays. There upon a barren heath the three weird sisters circle about their bubbling cauldron, tossing in all sorts of disgusting ingredients, and chanting and cackling while they contemplate the doom that is ultimately to overtake Macbeth and most of the other characters in the play.

Today we regard the scene as purely a product of the great playwright's imagination. But in the sixteenth century people believed in witchcraft and black magic. Shakespeare's witches with their ghastly brew and strange incantations were frighteningly real to men and women of sixteenth-century England and elsewhere.

*Macbeth and the three witches. Illustration from an early eighteenth-
century edition of Shakespeare's works.*

In his book *Witchcraft in the Middle Ages*, Professor James
Burton Russell states:

> To understand witchcraft we must descend into the
> darkness of the deepest oceans of the mind. In our efforts
> to avoid facing the realities of human evil, we have tamed
> the witch and made her comic, dressing her in a peaked
> cap and setting her on a broom for the amusement of
> children at Halloween. Thus made silly she can easily be
> exorcised from our minds, and we can convince children
> —and ourselves—that there is no such thing as a witch.
> But there is, or at least there was. A phenomenon that for
> centuries gripped the minds of men from the most
> illiterate peasant to the most skilled philosopher or
> scientist, imposing torture and death upon hundreds of
> thousands, is neither a joke nor illusion.

The subjects of witchcraft and magic are enormous. They involve
history, anthropology, religion, psychology, and, some would contend, psychic phenomena. We can't hope to summarize past and
present beliefs and theories about such subjects in a single chapter.
What we intend to do here is look at one aspect of the
phenomena—that of black magic, magic that was designed specifically to hurt people. To medieval man this was *maleficium,*
evildoing.

During the Middle Ages the Church officially made no distinction
between what we now call white magic, or helpful magic, and black
magic, or harmful magic. All magic was presumed to be accom-

plished with the aid of the Devil or lesser demons. Therefore, by definition, all magic was evil, since it involved invoking the powers of evil. In the orthodox view the witch who concocted a potion meant to cure a fever was just as bad as the witch who brewed a potion meant to cause a fever. Indeed, some Church authorities inclined toward the view that good witches were more dangerous than bad ones. Because their real evil—dealing with the Devil—was hidden by their benign magic, they could more easily lead men astray. Thus deceived, a man might endanger his immortal soul. A witch who placed a curse on an individual that caused him to die would only have harmed his body.

But the common people knew the difference. Except for the worst years of the antiwitchcraft hysteria, white witches or magicians were tolerated, even by the Church, while only the black witches or magicians were feared and persecuted.

The term black magic is really based upon a mistranslation. To the magicians of the ancient world, magic was neither bad nor good, neither black nor white. It was merely powerful. It could be used to hurt or help, as could any other force of nature. The attitude of the ancients toward magic was much the same as the modern attitude toward a force like electricity. Electricity is fine when it is used to light our homes, but not at all welcome if one happens to be sitting in the electric chair. The electricity itself, however, is entirely neutral.

Divination, that is, attempting to foretell the future, was an integral part of ancient magic. Divination in Greek is *manteia;* hence the suffix "mancy" is used in technical descriptions of divination. For example, "oneiromancy" is divination by dreams. The form of divination that nonmagicians regarded as the most unsavory was necromancy, the practice of digging up dead bodies and causing them to utter prophesies. This art was called "necromancy" from the Greek word *nekros,* meaning corpse. But when the term was translated into Latin the Greek word *nekros* was often confused with the Latin word *niger* for black. It was largely out of this confusion that the term "black magic" came to be applied to any fearful or harmful form of magic, while the word "necromancer" became a general term for "black magician."

Magic, as we said, is extremely ancient, and its forms have varied greatly from age to age and place to place. But there are a few basic magical principles that hold true for practically all forms of magic.

The first is what Sir James Frazer, in his pioneering book on anthropology, *The Golden Bough*, called "sympathetic magic." Sympathetic magic is divided into two branches. One branch, "imitative magic," is based on the belief that like produces like. The other branch, "contagious magic," is based on the belief that once things have been in contact, they retain a magical link.

A simple example of imitative magic is the so-called voodoo doll. (In fact, such dolls are not limited to voodoo; their use has been worldwide.) The magician makes an image of his intended victim and then sticks a pin into it. The victim is supposed to feel pain in a spot corresponding to the one pierced by the pin on the doll—like produces like. In practice the spell isn't usually that simple. There are a great many other things that the magician must do to make it work.

One of the things most often used to make the voodoo doll more effective is contagious magic. Thus, the magician may stuff his doll with bits of clothing recently worn by his intended victim or with scraps of the victim's fingernails or hair clippings. A few drops of the intended victim's blood is considered an exceptionally potent ingredient.

Throughout the centuries sympathetic magic has been applied in countless different ways. The basic magical operations have been vastly modified and elaborated upon and have been elevated into complicated rituals that may take hours or days to perform and involve a huge panoply of magical apparatus. Yet in even the most complex magical ritual these two simple procedures can often be recognized as the core of the operation.

Another important principle to understand about magic is the magician's belief in an animistic universe—that is, a universe which is alive. In the magician's view the universe is made up of forces, often personified as spirits, which control everything that happens. Not only do men have personal souls or spirits; so do animals, plants, rivers, rocks, the wind—practically anything you can name. Sometimes the spirits are general and undefined. At other times they are very specific and have names and distinct personalities. By

Yvonne of the School of Wicca, Salem, Missouri, demonstrates a "cross not my path" spell, designed to get rid of the unwanted attentions of another. This is the procedure: Arrange a wooden table where you will not be disturbed, and cover it with a linen cloth (1). Draw a large circle of sea salt on the cloth in a clockwise direction. In the center of the circle place a silver coin (dollar or fifty-cent piece) and on it a small red candle. Place nails at each of the cardinal points (2). As the moon crosses the meridian on the first night after it is new, write the name of the one to be discouraged on a piece of parchment in red ink using an old-fashioned nib pen. Draw the symbol of the sun above it and of the moon below it, then cross everything out with a single line. Turn off the lights and light the candle with a wooden match (3). Hold the paper in your hands. Look into the flame and think about what you wish to be done. When the candle is almost burnt out, burn the paper in it and cry in a loud voice, "By Aradia, (name of person), get thee gone and cross not my path." Take the ashes from the burnt paper and divide them into three parts. Place them in envelopes and mail them at nine-day intervals to the one whose name was burned. Say the instructions for the spell, "Unless it is the God's will for you to endure the person, you will never meet again."

1.

2.

3·

the use of his art the magician tries to control these spirits. The word "sorcerer," though now used as a synonym for magician, originally meant one who dealt with spirits.

The most common method of controlling the spirits, at least in the Western world, has been the practice of word magic. Words, particularly the names of the spirits themselves, used in incantations had unparalleled power. The word *incantantio* originally meant "chanting," came to mean "a spell," and has yielded our word "enchantment." Word magic is itself a form of sympathetic magic. In magical thinking the name becomes the thing, and saying a name gives the magician the same sort of power that possessing nail clippings or bits of hair would give.

All Western magic for the last fifteen hundred years has been powerfully influenced by the Cabala, a collection of Jewish magical and mystical lore. In the Cabala the word YHWH, the four transliterated Hebrew letters of the name of God, are used in the most powerful magical spells. Christian occultists have picked up the tradition and have added a host of other names as well. The nineteenth-century occultist and scholar of magic Eliphas Levi observed that in magic "to have said is to have done."

A more modern explanation of how spirits are attracted is given by Richard Cavendish in his book *The Black Arts.* "Concentration is essential. Occultists believe that the magician's will can be turned on to other people like a ray or beam. If he is projecting hatred or cruelty, evil spirits will be attracted by the current of force and will join the operation."

Once these spirits or forces are summoned they must be contained somehow. Just as an electrician may contain the force of electricity within a wire or a battery so the magician contains the powerful spiritual forces he has roused within a magically defined space—a pentacle or some other figure that has magical signifi-cance.

Symbolism is extremely important to magic. It was not pure theatricality that had Shakespeare put his witches on a barren heath with thunder and lightning in the background. If evil deeds were to be done, then the witch or magician should pick as evil a setting as possible in which to do them. Grimories, medieval books of magical formulas, often advise casting spells in the dark of the moon, traditionally an evil time, or at midnight, another time with evil associations. Often objects were used simply to invoke a particular aura. If the magician wished to cast a spell that would cause the death of someone, he might use the dust from a grave. All of the ingredients that Shakespeare's witches tossed into their cauldron, like fillet of snake and bat's wool, were ingredients that were associated with the powers of darkness and evil. The magician and witch used this sort of object for symbolic or dramatic effect. But in the world of magic symbolism and drama are a part of reality.

There is also a strong emotional element in magic. Magical rituals were rarely carried out with cool indifference. When casting a spell of revenge or hatred the magician really had to feel hatred and project this feeling into his spell as best he could.

As a society grows and changes, its magic tends to become more complex. Once simple magical rituals incorporate later beliefs and practices which often obscure the original logic behind the magical act. In some primitive hunting societies the shaman or tribal magician will stab the footprint of a game animal with a spear or transfix it with an arrow. This is a very obvious form of contagious magic. The belief is that stabbing the footprint made by the animal will make it easier for the hunters to catch that animal.

In a medieval grimory called the *Grimorium Varum* a ritual that has the same origin is recommended for disposing of an enemy, but it is no longer simple. According to the grimory you first dig up an old coffin in a graveyard and remove the nails from it while chanting, "Nails I take you that you may serve to turn aside and cause evil to all persons whom I will. In the name of the Father and the Son and the Holy Spirit." Then find a footprint that has been made by your enemy. Before driving one of the nails into the footprint, say, *"Pater noster upto in terra."* This is a parody of the Lord's Prayer meaning "Our father who art on earth," clearly an appeal to the Devil, who many medieval Europeans believed to be the lord of the earth. Drive the nail in with a rock and say, "Cause harm to (name of victim) until I remove thee."

In order to get rid of the spell one reverses the process by pulling the nail out while saying, "I remove thee so that the evil which thou hast caused to (name of victim) shall cease. In the name of the Father and of the Son and of the Holy Spirit. Amen."

The Christian elements were added because medieval Europeans, though they believed in magic, were also believing Christians, and adaptations of Christian rituals would seem to make any spell more powerful, even one invoking the Devil. The coffin nails suggest an aura of death and the graveyard, another element which would serve to multiply the power of this malignant spell.

A rather grisly magical implement that was reputed to have great powers was called the Hand of Glory. This was a hand cut from the corpse of a man who had died by hanging. A description of how to prepare the Hand of Glory is contained in a book called *Marvelous Secrets of Natural and Cabalistic Magic of Little Albert* published in 1722. According to Little Albert the hand should be wrapped in a piece of winding sheet and squeezed thoroughly so that all of the blood is drained out. The hand is then pickled for fifteen days in an earthenware jug with pepper, saltpeter, and something called zimort. Afterward it is dried in the heat of the sun during the period from July 3 to August 31. This is the period known as the dog days, because Sirius, the Dog Star, rises and sets with the sun. The sun is supposed to impart its light to the hand, while the influence of Sirius is supposed to make it more dangerous. It was once believed that the star contributed to causing rabies among dogs. If the hand is not yet sufficiently dried out it can be heated in a furnace.

Any fat which runs from the hand is saved and mixed with wax that is made into a candle and stuck between the fingers of the dead hand.

The deadness of the hand was supposed to be transmitted through the light of the candle to anyone who saw the light, and it was supposed either to kill or temporarily paralyze that person.

Occasionally robbers used such a hand as a protection against being interrupted at their work. Apparently it didn't always have the desired effect for there are some cases on record where burglars were captured while attempting to paralyze their victims with the light from a Hand of Glory.

This belief has been astonishingly persistent. As late as 1939 a gang of murderers in Philadelphia was found using a preserved human hand or a model of a human hand in order to terrify possible witnesses to their crimes.

No magic spell, no matter how powerful it was reputed to be and how perfectly it was carried out, was going to work unless the magician himself was in the proper state of readiness. In ancient times it was generally believed that not everyone possessed the power to become a magician, or at least that not everyone possessed the power in the same degree. In primitive societies the post of magician is often hereditary, the assumption being that magical power is hereditary. The truly great magicians of myth and history, like Merlin of the legends of King Arthur, were reputed to have had miraculous signs attend their births. Modern believers in magic no longer speak of a person's possessing "magical" powers, but rather of their having "psychic" powers. In practice these amount to pretty much the same thing.

Even the greatest magicians, however, could not work a difficult spell merely by waving a wand and uttering a few magic words. A careful and often lengthy period of preparation was necessary. The more awesome the spell, the more elaborate the preparation. A magician preparing for a difficult magical operation can be compared to an athlete in training for a big event.

The most common feature of any magical preparation is abstinence. The magician may withdraw from society for a period of time. Many spells require a prolonged abstinence from any sexual contact. An ancient and commonly used method of starting an evil chain of events against a particular individual is called the Black Fast. For a limited period of time the magician eats nothing or very little. Each time he refuses to eat a meal he thinks about the victim and repeats a curse to himself. The object of this is to store up and concentrate his magical energy for release against the victim at a specific time. The Black Fast is a reversal of the fasts which were regular features of Christian practice.

In 1538 an accused witch named Mabel Brigge was executed at York, England, after having confessed to killing a man by a Black Fast. She abstained from meat, milk, and all dairy foods and while doing so concentrated her hateful thoughts upon her victim.

These and other magical means come together in a magical extravaganza called the Operation of Grand Bewitchment. This operation is said by some to be the most ancient and most potent of all the rituals of destructive magic. Others scoff at it as a nonsensical collection of magical odds and ends cobbled together without any significant historical precedent. It is, say the critics, a foolish form of magical overkill. Whichever opinion is correct, the Operation of Grand Bewitchment is practically an encyclopedia of malevolent magic. A closer look at the ritual should give you a good idea of how various forms of black magic were, and occasionally still are, used in practice.

The magician prepares himself for the operation by a Black Fast. Then at midnight on a Tuesday night just before a new moon (a night near the winter solstice, the shortest day of the year, is best) the operation is begun.

The magician begins by drawing a triangle with one point aimed directly northward on the floor. Inside the triangle he puts the wax or clay that he is going to use later in the operation. The outside of the triangle is wreathed with various winter plants like evergreens and holly, plus any horned skulls, like goat or ram skulls, that he happens to have. The first part of the operation is aimed at invoking a spirit for the spell. Any one of a number of demons can be used. Some modern magicians express a preference for the spirit of a horned Celtic god called Cernunnos, who is, in one aspect at least, identified with the god of war Mars and with the spirits of destruction and revenge.

One way to invoke Cernunnos is by using the Square of Mars, which is a series of numbers written thus:

11	24	7	20	3
4	12	25	8	16
17	5	13	21	9
10	18	1	14	22
23	6	19	2	15

The Square of Mars is a mathematical oddity in which all the lines, vertical and horizontal, add up to 65. Since at least the time of the ancient Greeks, numbers were believed to have magical significance. Numerical oddities like the one above were often called "magic squares." Just how this one became connected with Mars or Cernunnos is unknown.

While writing out the magic square the magician is supposed to keep images of war and destruction in his mind and chant names which conjure up such images. He may, for example, chant the names of the war gods of various ancient peoples: "Thunor, Balor,

Costume of the horned god of the witches, supposedly worn by the grand master of a witch coven. The model is on display in the witchcraft museum on the Isle of Man.

Ares, Mars!" Or a more up-to-date magician could chant a word that has come to signify the terrifying destruction of war: "Hiroshima! Hiroshima! Hiroshima!"

In preparing this magic square the magician is supposed to work himself up to a frenzy so as to transmit the proper emotion or force into the square. It is a most exhausting task.

In medieval times the magician expected the demon to appear in person, but the modern magician is usually satisfied by meditating upon the square until the image of Cernunnos is fixed firmly in his mind. After this is done the triangle on the floor is consecrated with bitter wine while the magician chants, "Eko, Eko, Azarak," etc.

Bitter herbs and dust from a grave are ground up with a mortar and pestle and placed in the triangle while the magician chants rhythmically: "I work to the destruction of (victim's name)! I work to the destruction of (victim's name)!"

The next stage of the operation involves making an image or puppet from wax or clay. The model should be from five to eight inches long. While it is being made the magician should chant the name of the victim over and over. Fingernail clippings, hair, or blood from the victim, if available, are to be mixed in with the clay or wax. Some modern witches or magicians will also incorporate a photograph of the intended victim in the model. When the magician feels that the puppet is ready he engraves the name of the victim in the soft material while chanting, "Cabye. Aaaze. Hit. Fel Meltat."

The magician then fixes an image of the victim in his mind, consecrates the image by dabbing it with the bitter wine, and chants:

"In the name of Cernunnos the Horned One creature of wax (or clay) I name thee (name of victim). Thou art (name of victim)!"

A few more ritual acts are performed with the puppet, then it is placed in the center of the triangle with its head pointing north.

Now the magician takes a scarlet candle, called a candle of bewitchment, and anoints it with magical oil while chanting a litany of hate and destruction in which he specifies the exact torment he wishes the victim to undergo. This chant must be repeated many times. Some magical texts suggest eighty-one repetitions while others recommend even more.

The candle is then placed at the north point of the triangle and lit. Then comes a vital part of the ritual: The magician removes the blame for the crime that he is about to commit from himself to the spirit of Cernunnos. In a sense he becomes Cernunnos for the balance of the operation. Standing at the north end of the triangle, he crosses his arms over his breast and chants: "It is not my hand which does this deed, but that of Cernunnos, the Horned One."

From this point onward the magician is supposed to be completely under the control of the horned god. He grasps a specially consecrated needle in his left hand and chants a long Latin incantation which goes in part:

> *Arator, Lapidator, Omtator!*
> *Somniator, Subaerfor, Iquator!*
> *Signator, Sudator, Combustor!*
> *Comestor, Onerator!*

Now the magician, controlled by the horned Cernunnos, viciously stabs the puppet in the spot where harm is intended while uttering the words, "So mote it be!" If the magician wishes his victim to waste slowly away, rather than to suffer an affliction of any single part of his body, then he takes the needle, stabs the puppet through the heart, and melts it in a fire if it is made of wax, or dissolves it in water if it is made of clay.

The spell is completed when the candle of bewitchment burns itself out.

This is a long and extremely complicated spell. I have given only the highlights of the ritual here. If it fails and the intended victim continues to prosper rather than falling ill or dying, the magician can find a thousand reasons why the spell has gone wrong. Perhaps some part of the ritual has been improperly performed. Indeed, it is difficult to imagine how such a long and complicated ritual could be performed correctly in every detail. Perhaps some of the ingredients used were impure, or possibly the intended victim has worked a form of countermagic. Failure does not mean that the magician has to question the power of magic. Instead, failure drives the magician to try again. Perhaps next time he will get it right. However, if the victim does suffer in any way after the spell is performed, then belief in magic is confirmed. One apparent success can wash away the memory of a thousand failures. Magic, like most other systems of belief, is self-confirming. Once one accepts its basic principles, everything can be explained within the system.

When plucked from its belief system, the Operation of Grand Bewitchment sounds childish and almost funny. If the average person today were to encounter someone trying to perform this ritual in his cellar or living room he would be inclined to regard the person as mad rather than powerful and the ritual as more foolish than frightening. But this ritual and others like it do not come out of a twentieth-century view of the world. Modern practitioners of magic tend to stress the "psychic" side of the practice. They say that all the implements and chanting and the rest have no power in themselves, but are merely methods of helping to focus "psychic" power.

This modern explanation, however, lacks conviction. A presumed belief in psychic powers is a slender thread upon which to hang all the elaborate paraphernalia and ritual of the Operation of Grand Bewitchment or any other magical spell. As a result, those who profess to be practitioners of magic and casters of spells in the twentieth century appear more eccentric and even clownish than sinister. But it is wrong to try to judge the power of beliefs of a past age by the standards of the present.

In a time when everyone, as Professor Russell says, "from the most illiterate peasant to the most skilled philosopher or scientist" accepted a magical view of the world, there was nothing amusing about a spell like the Operation of Grand Bewitchment. A person who knew that someone reputed to be a powerful magician had worked such an awesome and terrible spell against him might actually feel pain, might even sicken and die, just as the magician had expected him to.

Today we would put such a reaction down to the power of suggestion, for we do know that suggestion can have a devastating effect upon human beings. We are at a loss to explain exactly how such a power works, but we know that it does. Physicians who deal with critically ill patients are familiar with what is called "the will to live." A patient who sincerely believes that he is going to recover actually has a better chance of recovering than someone in an identical physical state who has given up hope. A careless word by a doctor or relative may send a sick man into a relapse.

No amount of "will to live" is going to cause a terminal cancer patient to recover, nor will fear of death make a common cold into a life-threatening illness. But there is a vast area between these two extremes where suggestion or belief can play an important role.

Can one say that suggestion is "magic"? Not really. There is an important qualitative difference between this psychological explanation of why spells sometimes have the intended effect and the explanation offered by believers in magic, even the modern psychically-oriented magicians. The magicians see the power of the spell coming directly from the rituals and the implements or from some force that emanates from the body or mind of the magician. The psychologist views things the other way round. He says that the real power of the spell is not in the magician, but in the mind of the victim, and that if one does not believe in magic no spell, no matter how carefully performed, will have any effect.

If one wishes to be truly modern in one's approach to magic it should be possible, by using the magical principles outlined in this chapter, to create spells more suitable to the twentieth century than the eye of newt, toe of frog, dark of the moon spells popular in Shakespeare's day. Here is a spell that I devised for my own amusement:

At five o'clock on a weekday afternoon go to any busy intersection where there is a traffic jam. Cars will be belching an exceptionally high level of exhaust fumes into the already polluted atmosphere. Take a photograph of your intended victim, crumple it up, and throw it viciously into the already littered gutter. Step on it until it is thoroughly smeared with grime and filth. Then take a phial of dirty water drawn from a nearby polluted river and pour it slowly over the picture while chanting, "Choke! Choke! Choke!" If the principles of magic are correct, your victim should begin to gag and choke almost immediately.

VII - AMULETS AND TALISMANS

Three Rings for the Elven-kings under the sky,
Seven for the Dwarf-lords in their halls of stone,
Nine for Mortal Men doomed to die,
One for the Dark Lord on his dark throne.
—J. R. R. Tolkien, The Lord of the Rings

THE WORLD of primitive man was not only filled with a host of real dangers—starvation, disease, wild animals, violent enemies, etc.—there was also the invisible world of evil spirits and the machinations of hostile sorcerers to contend with. To protect himself from his visible enemies a man might carry a weapon. To protect himself from invisible enemies he would carry another sort of weapon, a small object that has been called an amulet or talisman.

Everybody used these objects to one degree or another. Sir E. A. Wallis Budge wrote:

> In every place in our own country and in foreign lands where excavations on the sites of ancient cities have been made, the spade of the excavator has brought to light a number of objects of various kinds and sizes which we may call generally Amulets and Talismans, and regard as the works of men who were believers in Magic. The use of these objects was not confined to any one place, or

people, or period, and the great mass of the evidence about the matter now available justified the statement that the use of amulets and talismans was, and it may be added, still is, universal. We may even go further and say that it is coeval with the existence of *Homo sapiens* on earth.

To find out about the use of these protective objects in the modern world we do not have to go to the reports of anthropologists who study the customs of tiny tribes on remote Pacific islands. All we have to do is look around us. From the rabbit's foot or lucky coin that many carry in their pockets to the plastic saint with a magnetic base stuck upon the dashboard of many cars, we are still trying to protect ourselves from evil through the use of amulets and talismans.

Perhaps the most familiar use of an object to ward off evil is displayed in the movie *Dracula* and other vampire movies. The monster is approaching his victim when the victim suddenly holds up a cross. The vampire reels back, shielding his eyes from the hated sight, and disappears. The scene is a fictional creation, but as a dramatic example it is effective. The physical symbol of goodness drives away the presence of evil.

While learned theologians would have asserted that the cross, religious medals, and statues and relics of saints were not magical objects, common folk often treated them as such. People wore crosses and religious medals in the belief that these objects offered supernatural protection against the machinations of the Devil and of the witches and evil sorcerers who were the Devil's agents.

The borderline between Christianity and magic, particularly during the Middle Ages, was at best a hazy one. As we have seen it was quite usual for sorcerers to use ordinary Christian prayers as part of their magical spells. Likewise, it was common for the makers of amulets and talismans to use religious objects. One of the most frequently used charms in Europe for many centuries was simply a bit of paper inscribed with a fragment of a Latin prayer and worn around the neck. This was considered an excellent protection against disease, as well as against black magic. In fact, there was little difference, since many people believed that disease was caused by black magic.

Earlier peoples had worn or carried representations of their gods as protection against evil. The Hebrews, however, were forbidden by strict biblical injunction from making graven images. Yet many Hebrews, especially those under the influence of the mystical Cabala, made a huge variety of amulets which contained Hebrew letters, symbols, and numbers, all of which were believed to have magical significance.

The Cabala, which was a sophisticated and complicated work, was very attractive to Christian occultists and magical thinkers from the time of the Renaissance onward. During the sixteenth century Cornelius Agrippa, one of history's most learned magical theoreticians, included numerous examples of cabalistic amulets in his massive work on magic, *Occult Philosophy.*

A simple amulet cited by Agrippa was intended to protect the wearer from earthquakes, baleful devils, and wicked men. On one side are the Hebrew letters for BWWWW and on the other SMDBH. These are the initial and final letters of the first five verses of the book of Genesis in Hebrew. Just why this particular set of letters was considered protective is a mystery locked deep within cabalistic speculations, but the point is that this sort of protective amulet was common among both Christians and Jews interested in the more esoteric kinds of magic.

Crosses or cabalistic symbols are man-made objects supposedly infused with some sort of magical or divine protective power. But there is another form of amulet said to protect the wearer from evil

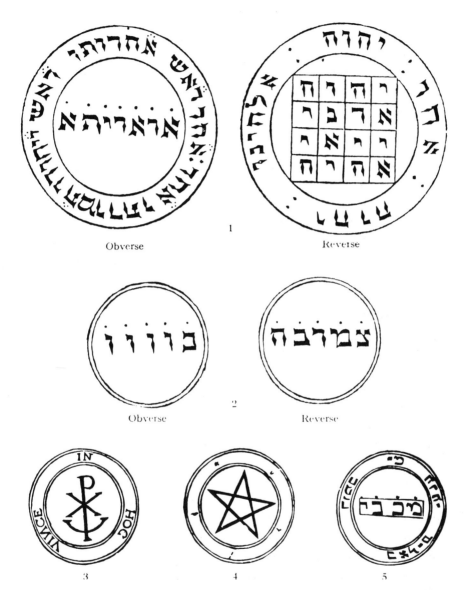

Hebrew and Christian amulets. No. 2 was intended to protect the wearer from earthquakes, baleful devils, and wicked men.

influences. These are natural objects that operate through their own inherent magical properties.

Various types of minerals, usually precious stones, were regarded as having significant magical power. Often the stone itself, or the stone used in conjunction with other materials, made a protective amulet. Among the uneducated a jewel might be considered a powerful amulet merely because it was valuable or pretty, but to one learned in the secrets of magic, jewels and other natural objects contained specific magical properties related to their specific characteristics.

To people today the most familiar of these natural amulets are the so-called birthstones. These are minerals, which are supposed to be worn in rings or lockets, that will attract good luck and ward off evil influences. There is a particular mineral for persons born under each sign of the zodiac. Modern astrologers do not take the birthstone idea as seriously as astrologers once did, and the lists of which stone is related to which sign vary considerably from place to place. Such lists are usually prepared by jewelers rather than astrologers.

Modern astrologers generally lack the sweeping cosmological vision possessed by astrologers of the sixteenth and seventeenth centuries. At that time astrology was merely one part of a complete magical view of the universe. This view is expressed best in the phrase "As above, so below." This implies an elaborate system of correspondence between everything in nature. The movements of the planets affect the lives of human beings, but the planets also affect specific parts of the body, certain diseases, plants, and minerals. Thus a ring of a particular type might be used to attract certain planetary influences and help protect the wearer from evil. Jewelry made under astrological principles was believed to be particularly effective in warding off or curing disease—which many felt was due to planetary influences.

One Renaissance authority suggested that rings intended to attract the influence of certain planets be made of the following materials:

Sun   Diamond or topaz set in gold.
Moon   Pearl, crystal, or quartz set in silver.
Mercury   Opal or agate set in quicksilver.
Venus   Emerald or turquoise set in copper.
Mars   Ruby or any red stone set in iron.
Jupiter   Sapphire, amethyst, or cornelian set in tin.
Saturn   Onyx or sapphire set in lead.

From this list one can get a glimpse into the logic behind the magical world of correspondences. Diamond, topaz, and gold were considered "fiery" materials and corresponded with the sun. Pearl, crystal, quartz, and silver are "pale" materials and corresponded with the pale moon. The planet Mars has a faintly reddish glow when viewed with the naked eye and was identified with red stones. Mars is also the god of war, and the redness of blood reinforces the identification. Iron ore is reddish, and iron turns reddish with rust. Iron is also the metal most closely identified with war, hence with Mars.

The rings described above are very simple astrological talismans. The complexities possible in making an astrological amulet or talisman are almost infinite. Julianus Ristorus, professor at Pisa University in the early sixteenth century, owned a ring which had been engraved with certain characters when the moon was at mid-sky and "strong" in Cancer. This he used to cure ailments of the feet. He had another astrological ring designed especially to protect him from mosquitoes.

A fourteenth-century French archbishop was forced to resign when it was discovered that he had a Jewish astrologer carve astrological symbols into his pastoral rings. The symbols were supposed to ward off disease.

Though amulets and talismans were generally designed to be protective, some could be used with hostile intent. The early nineteenth-century English occultist Francis Barret suggested in his book *The Magus or Celestial Intelligencer* that a talisman made of lead and engraved when the moon was adversely aspected could be buried near a house and bring extreme ill fortune to those living in the house.

On a more mundane level an herb like garlic was supposed to ward off a variety of evil influences, including vampires, simply because it had a strong odor and flavor. If it was strong in one respect it should be strong in others, like driving off evil.

In the fourteenth century a man named Robert Tresillan was condemned to be hanged for treason. While on the scaffold he foolishly announced that he could not die so long as he kept his clothes on. The executioners accordingly deprived him of his clothes and found upon his person talismans painted "like unto the signs of heaven" (the signs of the zodiac) and the head of a devil and the names of devils painted on parchment. They took away the talismans and hanged Tresillan naked. He died.

During the witchcraft trials it was regular practice to strip and shave an accused witch during an interrogation. After about the fifteenth century the reason given for this practice was that the inquisitors were looking for a "Devil's mark," a mark supposedly made by the Devil when he signed a pact with a witch in order to brand the witch as his subject. But before the fifteenth century the practice was already in use, though at that time the stated reason was that the inquisitors were looking for diabolic amulets or talismans the witch might have concealed.

As we said, the power attributed to amulets and talismans is not as great today as it once was, primarily because the whole elaborate

A gesture of benediction becomes one of malediction when one looks at the shadow which reproduces the profile of the Devil. The drawing is supposed to show the two-sided nature of all things.

system of magical thinking is not as popular as it once was. When modern occultists are asked to account for the effectiveness of such objects they are more likely to respond that the amulets or talismans have no power in themselves. Instead, they help the magician or the astrologer or the occultist "focus his psychic powers" in much the same way as the wax doll or magic circle helps the magician to focus those powers.

The host of lucky charms or good luck pieces that we carry around with us are little more than the relics of superstition. Superstition, says Professor Russell, is a belief "not consistent with a coherent view of the world." To the astrologer or the magician, who

saw the universe as one vast system of interlocking correspondences, the wearing of an iron ring to attract the influence of Mars,
or even the use of garlic to ward off evil spirits, would not have been
a superstition. Such an act fit their particular view of the universe.
But when a twentieth-century person carries about a rabbit's foot or
a lucky coin in the belief that this will attract something called luck
or ward off bad luck, that is indeed a superstitious act.

SUGGESTIONS FOR FURTHER READING

Barber, Richard and Riches, Anne. *A Dictionary of Fabulous Beasts*. New York: Walker, 1971.

Baring-Gould, Sabine. *Curious Myths of the Middle Ages*. London: Longmans, Green, 1897.

Budge, E. A. Wallis. *Amulets and Talismans*. New York: University Books, 1961.

Cavendish, Richard. *The Black Arts*. New York: Putnam's, 1967.

Christian, Paul. *The History and Practice of Magic*. New York: Citadel, 1963.

Cohen, Daniel. *Voodoo, Devils and the New Invisible World*. New York: Dodd, Mead, 1972.

Dale-Green, Patricia. *Cult of the Cat*. Boston: Houghton Mifflin, 1963.

De Camp, L. Sprage and De Camp, Catherine. *Spirits, Stars and Spells*. New York: Canaveral Press, 1966.

Goodwin, John. *This Baffling World*. New York: Hart Publishing, 1968.

Hill, Douglas and Williams, Pat. *The Supernatural*. New York: Hawthorn, 1966.

Hole, Christina. *Witchcraft in England*. New York: Scribners, 1947.

Holzer, Hans. *The Habsburg Curse*. New York: Doubleday, 1972.

Howley, W. Oldfield. *The Cat in the Mysteries of Magic and Religion*. New York: Castle Books, 1956.

Hudson, Paul. *Mastering Witchcraft*. New York: Putnam's, 1971.

Keel, John A. *UFOs Operation Trojan Horse*. New York: Putnam's, 1970.

Robbins, Rossell Hope. *The Encyclopedia of Witchcraft and Demonology.* New York: Crown, 1959.

Russell, Jeffrey Burton. *Witchcraft in the Middle Ages.* Ithaca: Cornell University Press, 1972.

Sanderson, Ivan. *Invisible Residents.* New York: World, 1970.

Spence, Lewis. *Encyclopedia of Occultism.* New York: University Books, 1960.

Thomas, Keith. *Religion and the Decline of Magic.* New York: Scribners, 1971.

INDEX

ABOUT THE AUTHOR

DANIEL COHEN, journalist and former editor of *Science Digest*, has always had an interest in the bizarre and occult, as well as in the natural sciences. He has written several books on occult subjects—including MAGICIANS, WIZARDS, & SORCERERS; A NATURAL HISTORY OF UNNATURAL THINGS; IN SEARCH OF GHOSTS; and THE MAGIC ART OF FORESEEING THE FUTURE—and has appeared widely on radio and television. Mr. Cohen is a native of Chicago and holds a degree in journalism from the University of Illinois. He lives with his wife and daughter and a collection of cats and dogs in Port Jervis, New York.